TALE OF THE

GATOR

TALE OF THE

GATOR

The Story of

CRAIG BODZIANOWSKI

The Boxer Who Wouldn't Stay Down

by

Craig Bodzianowski
&
Mike Fitzgerald

Published by Lemieux International, Ltd.
P. O. Box 170134
Milwaukee, Wisconsin 53217-8011
Cover design by Michael Olive
Manufactured in the United States of America
ISBN 0-9667269-6-0

Catologing in Publication Data

Bodzianowski, Craig, (date)-
Tale of the gator : the story of Craig Bodzianowski, the boxer who wouldn't stay down /
by Craig Bodzianowski & Mike Fitzgerald.
p.cm.
ISBN 0-9667269-6-0 (pbk.)
1. Bodzianowski, Craig, (date)- 2. Boxers (Sports)—United States—Biography. 3.Physically handicapped athletes—United States—Biography. I. Title: Story of Craig Bodzianowski, the boxer who wouldn't stay down.. II. Fitzgerald, Mike, (date)- III. Title.

GV1132.B58 A3 2000
796.83'092—dc21
[B]

00-048761

Dedication

"This book is dedicated to my Mom and Dad, to brother Billy my first role model, to Mr. O'Connor and Mr. Nate Bolden who came to be part of my family, to my nephew Jeffry and all the friends and family who stood by me in the difficult days. They are the true heroes of this story."

—Craig Bodzianowski

"To my mentors: Phil Gatewood and Marshall Terrill. Phil, thanks for all your help in the investigation industry; and Marshall, thanks for the vote of confidence for this book and opening the doors for other books."

—Mike Fitzgerald

ACKNOWLEDGEMENTS

To write a book takes many people who work behind the scenes to help the author tell a story. I would like to gratefully acknowledge the following for their contributions:

Jerry Lenza, his wife Bennie, and son Don. I met at the Lenza household for several interviews. I could always count on an excellent Italian meal and many stories on the Gator. Jerry and I have been in continuous contact since the beginning of the project. Without him, this book would not have happened.

Special thanks to "Iron" Mike Friedel for convincing Craig to allow me to write his life story.

I would also like to thank boxing journalist and historian Pete Ehrmann for editing the original manuscript and for his suggestions along the way. And also a special thank you to Julie-Burke-Seymour for her help in the editing process.

A heartfelt thank you to all the members of the Bodzianowski family who contributed in so many ways to the making of this book, especially to Gloria (Mom), Donna and Jeffry DeBauche.

A special thanks to Daniel "Rudy" Ruettiger for writing the Foreword, to John White for the cover photo, and to all those who contributed their comments throughout the book: Archie Moore, Don Lee, LeeRoy Murphy, Jerry Lenza, Sean O'Grady, Mary Hajduk, Mike Moe, Dave Tiberi, Frank Glienna, Jack Cowen, Ernie Terrell, Alfozno Ratliff, Bobby Hitz, and Don Poggi.

A sincere thank you to Mike Olive for his skillful handling of the cover art and photos, and to my editor William Lemieux for his excellent editorial contributions. Many thanks to Barbara Olive and David Subat, whose hard work behind the scenes went into the endeavor of making this a great book.

My parents, Mike and Claudia Fitzgerald have always been there for me. My wife, Debra has also been there for me and showed infinite patience with me as I pursued my passion of boxing.

EDITOR'S NOTE

Craig Bodzianowski is an ordinary man who through an act of fate was forced to confront an extraordinary circumstance. Ordinary does not mean common; nor does it mean like everyone else. What it means is that Craig possesses those characteristics which we most admire in men. He is one marked as possessing the best of them.

Many men have become athletes through perseverance and hard work. Some have had to overcome great obstacles. Craig has done both. As a result, he speaks with his life of what is most noble in the human experience.

When asked to facilitate and edit this book, I knew little about boxing and a lot about editing. I had worked with books that told the stories of World War II heroes, of family members who bore the pain of bereavement, as well as books that in episodic form laid out life's most poignant experiences. I expected this book would be like the others and fall someplace in between. I was wrong.

As I was introduced to Craig through his story, and was made aware of the twists and turns of his life, I met a truly great human being—a monumental man. Through his plain-spoken words, given to Mike Fitzgerald, I discovered that in these pages Craig has presented the honesty of a life well lived.

The Chinese say that life is not always measured by its final victory, but rather through the winning steps that in themselves create the ultimate success. In Craig's life, success is not the final title, but the journey in faith and courage that provided him the opportunity to try for the *golden ring.*

Craig minces no words. From the pitbulls, his father's temper, and his own shortcomings, Craig, in unique episodes, shows us how he came to be the man that he is. Thus he shows us why he himself is not and has never been disabled. Rather, he is enabled by a force of will which takes adversity and turns it into opportunity.

History shows us that human greatness is best found in ordinary men who face extraordinary circumstances, and because of their character rise to the occasion.

In showing us how his character was formed, Craig gives us a picture of both hard love and gentle caring from his parents. We follow his childhood foibles, his adolescent meandering, and his discovery of boxing as a voice of expression. When we understand Craig's roots, it is no surprise that Craig's Mom proudly sits ringside, and it is no surprise that the loss of his brother Billy would so dramatically propel him toward becoming the man that he is.

The best of a man; traits of loyalty, trust, courage, will, determination—they are all here. But more than these, the single-minded drive that called out crowds to shout "Gator" can be felt and understood.

Craig is the kind of man that a man would be honored to have as a friend. As shown in his story, he is not one who would forget those whose lives helped to build his successes.

Yes, I learned about boxing in this book. More importantly, I learned about the boxer's world, his feelings, needs, and desires. I learned a lot more. I also learned the true meaning of the word *will;* the *will* to persevere against all odds, the *will* to obtain the opportunity of a dream, the *will* to do one's best. All these add up to the *will* that propelled one man to rise above a tragic accident and to stand up for all men whom the world has listed as disabled.

Craig makes no excuses for himself. He does not curse the fates for their dark hand in his accident. He takes full responsibility for the ride that caused his injury, and in turn, full responsibility for the fight that allowed him to continue as a boxer. In telling his story, Craig does not place himself on a pedestal as one better than those around him. Instead he demonstrates what it means to be the crown of a wave propelled forward by the circumstances, family and friends that shared the formation of his life.

Yes, this is a book about boxing. The pictures of the fights are vivid and clear, and one can almost smell the scents that surround the ring. But that is only part of this book. The other part pushes out between the fights and among the struggles. It is the story of a man who discovered a greatness that carried him, against all adversity, into the ring to achieve his dream to be a boxer. It is the story of how he stayed there even after he lost his leg. Most of all it is a story that calls to the rest of us that as ordinary people we should also reach out toward the dreams of our lives. It calls out for our own need to achieve greatness by giving us in snippets and pieces a picture of a man who has clearly demonstrated that he is a great man; and, yes, still one of us.

On completion, I realized I've done more than edit a book in these pages. I have met a man who calls out to my better self, and I'm proud to be able to have a part in sharing his story. Thank you Craig for what you have given me.

Wm. F. Lemieux

William F. Lemieux

FOREWORD

Craig "The Gator" Bodzianowski is a man of my own heart. His never-give-up attitude allowed him to rise above his own limitations to become a world title contender, a word class athlete, and an inspiration to many.

Craig used the same positive attitude and game plan for winning at life that I used to make my dreams come true at the University of Notre Dame and with my movie "Rudy". In following the story of Craig "The Gator" Bodzianowski, I realize that he applied several of the positive beliefs that I have chronicled in my motivational book Rudy's Rules.

Craig suffered a setback which required a great deal of sacrifice to overcome. He eliminated all excuses and accepted the responsibility it would take to resume his professional boxing career despite losing his right foot and part of his right leg. Craig decided he wanted to be a championship caliber fighter and went out and did it. He was surrounded by many: his family, friends, coaches, and fans, who all wanted him to succeed and they supported him in his professional endeavors.

Craig worked hard, realizing there was no such thing as an over achiever. He dug down deep, willing to pay the price it took in order to compete again as a successful professional boxer. The word quit is not a part of his vocabulary.

Craig Bodzianowski has been an inspiration to many. He is a special person, and it is a pleasure to write the introduction to his story.

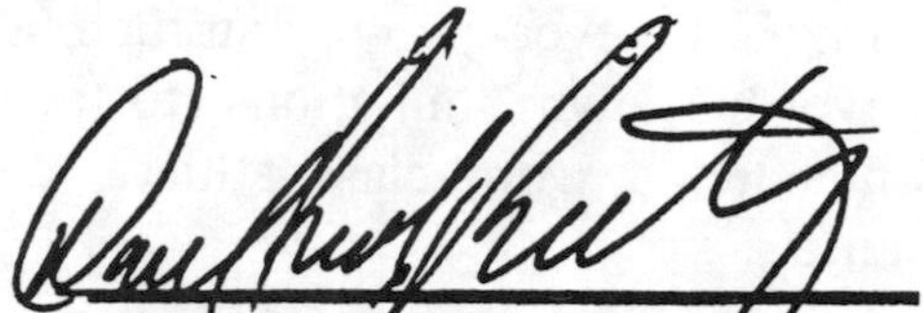

Daniel "Rudy" Ruettiger

PROLOGUE

It all happened so fast. One day I find out my fight manager verbally closes a deal for me to fight a former world champion on national television. The next day I lay in a hospital bed with my boxing career presumably over and facing the amputation of my right foot.

I was ecstatic beyond belief when my manager, Jerry Lenza, called from Atlantic City to announce that a nationally televised fight against ex-world champion, Mike Rossman, looked like a done deal. This was the opportunity I had been dreaming about. At the time, I was an unbeaten cruiserweight prospect with quite a following in the Chicago area. I was ready for the big time, and this seemed to be the big break. I knew that I had all the marketable qualities a modern 1980's boxer needed. I was white, bright, and could fight. Rossman was a former champion who needed a victory over a quality opponent. I was definitely the wrong opponent for a guy in his situation. His name would look great on my boxing resume. He was known for his guts and fighting heart, but I knew nobody could out-will me in a fight. I was excited about this opportunity. I kicked the "For Sale" sign off my Kawasaki 440 motorcycle and jumped on for one last ride to go see my good buddy, Bill Donne,. I stopped by to pick up my girlfriend, Beth Anderson, and off we went on the twenty-minute ride to the Chicago suburb of Olympia Fields.

I never should have climbed back on that damned cycle. It was clean, shined-up, and just about sold. A high school kid had stopped by and put a decent bid on it. It was an offer I had planned to accept. Jerry and my dad, Pat Bodzianowski, had been riding my ass hard to get rid of my favorite toy. They had both been on my case non-stop since I bought it. My old man was always griping to me about my bike, saying that I had too much to risk with my professional boxing career. Looking back, I should have given in to their wishes. But at the time I thought there could be no harm in one last spin on my Kawasaki.

After a brief visit with Bill, Beth and I headed back home. I was just two blocks away when the vehicle in front of me slowed down to turn. I passed the car on the left side, but it suddenly turned towards me. I had only a few precious seconds to think of a way to prevent the inevitable collision. I tried to steer the cycle out of harm's way but it was no good.

My cycle was hit and the next thing I remember was being flat on my back in the middle of the street. My first thought was Beth. Where was she? Was she O.K.? I looked around to find her and she seemed shaken but fine. She suffered only a few scratches and was able to walk away from the accident under her own power. I attempted to gain my own footing, but immediately crashed back to the ground. I could not believe this was happening to me. It seemed like a bad dream. One minute I was on top of the world. An hour later I lay there with my professional boxing career seemingly over, and looking at the amputation of my right foot. Talk about having your world turned upside down. I had no idea that one final ride would turn my world into a living nightmare. But there I was, in my hospital bed, staring at the ceiling and trying to make sense of the most traumatic experience of my life.

The accident could not have occurred at a worse time. I was making my move to the top. I had knocked out ten opponents along the way and had a record of thirteen victories without a defeat. I was now the featured fighter on Chicago-area boxing cards. I had a fan club and fight purses were increasing with every bout. My name now appeared in the Chicago newspapers more and more. People were starting to notice me wherever I went. Often I was addressed solely by my nickname, "Gator," which I earned in high school by tattooing an Izod brand name alligator on my left breast. Boxing promoters considered me a big box-office attraction thanks to my entertaining and aggressive fighting style. I was the man on top of the world until May 31, 1984. That's when the world, my dream, and my motorcycle all crashed together.

My new world, there on that street, was filled with pain. Once again I attempted to get up, and again collapsed in a heap. When I looked down to see what was keeping me there, I realized I was in deep trouble. Blood was everywhere, several of my bones were sticking out in all directions, and my right foot was pointing in the opposite direction from the rest of me. My first reaction was to pound the ground with my fist and yell, "Damn it! This can't be happening! What about my boxing career?" I screamed this at the top of my lungs along with a few other choice words. Although I never lost consciousness, everything that happened there was a surreal blur. I remember getting in the ambulance, and while I was on my way to the hospital I remember thinking how upset my parents would be, especially my old man. He was the one I had learned, at an early age, not to upset. I kept thinking about what he would say all the way to the hospital. When I got there, I did not want my parents to be notified of the accident. I had the utmost respect for my father. I knew how angry he would be once he found out. He was the only guy I knew who could put my undefeated record in jeopardy!

Of course, I couldn't stop thinking about my boxing career either. Fighting was what I did best. My goal was to compete for a world title. I loved to fight. This was the first time in my life that the thought of not being able to box actually crossed my mind. Before, I just naturally assumed that I would fight forever, or at least until I decided to stop. A world ranking was just around the corner. My professional boxing career just couldn't be over, I thought. Not yet. What else did I know?

ONE

Gloria Bodzianowski: *"Of all my children, Craig cried the least if at all. We did not have room for crybabies in our household. I remember one time I came home and there was blood everywhere. I didn't know what happened. I followed the trail of blood and it led to Craig. He was about seven at the time. He was sitting on the couch watching Bozo the Clown holding his thumb with a paper towel wrapped around it. Blood was dripping out on the floor. His cut would require several stitches, but he was afraid to tell anyone because he didn't want to get in trouble. Instead, he sat there with his thumb half cut off, not speaking a word. All my kids were tough, but Craig was extra tough."*

Because we lived in such cramped quarters, my parents had no tolerance for whiny or weepy kids. I learned early in life not to cry. We were taught at an early age not to start trouble, but to stand our ground and fight if trouble came our way. My dad instilled in us an attitude that kept us fighting no matter what. He felt that if a man gives up once, he'll give up again and again. He said the same was true of his pit bulls. Once one of them quit in a fight, it was never the same, because it had lost its fighting spirit. Dad made sure his children were full of fighting spirit.

When I was growing up, our house included an enclosed kennel where the pit bulls my dad raised and trained resided. It was a ten-by-twenty foot closed-in area that also served as my personal boxing ring where any challenger was welcome.

My dad must have been a zoo-keeper in a previous life. His hobby was animals—expecially fighting dogs. Pit bulls were his specialty. We always had between thirty and fifty fighting dogs along with a wide variety of other animals in our household. At various times, in addition to the dogs, we had goats, monkeys, piranhas, birds, and once even a 13-foot-long anaconda.

One day, a customer of my dad's named Eli Bush was over at the house checking on some pit bulls that he was looking to purchase. I was only about seven then, and all the fighting I had done up to that time was with my brothers or on the school playground. Eli knew my dad was a former boxer, and he brought along a pair of boxing gloves to give him. My father used these gloves to teach us how to box. With six kids in the family we had an ample number of sparring partners. My sister, Donna, may have been the toughest Bodzianowski of them all. Lucky for me, we never came to blows! Billy was the oldest child followed by my sisters, Denise and Donna. Then came me, followed by brothers, Howard and Ken.

My parents were married and ready to raise a family when they were only sixteen. (When I was sixteen, my only concerns were the next Golden Gloves bout, girls, and time out to look for trouble.) My parents met on a school bus. They both attended Wescott Vocational High in the heart of Chicago. The day they met Mom followed Dad home and bought him a Coke. The rest was history. They had six children by the time they were twenty-five, and their marriage lasted thirty-eight years until my father's death in 1993. Mom never worked outside the home. Working outside the home was not even an option for her, because Dad felt a woman's place was in the home. Her full-time job was raising us. Talk about a job with lots of overtime! Mom didn't even have a driver's license until a few years ago.

Each of us provided his own separate challenge for her. If it were not for me, Mom never would have gotten on a first-name basis with our principal. My juvenile conduct never ceased to amaze my mom. The other Bodzianowski children weren't always easy to handle either, but Mom did a decent job of parenting.

Dad worked an assortment of jobs to put food on the table. At one time or another, he was in construction, produce, and did factory work. Eventually he found employment in the tattooing industry. He supplemented his income by training and selling pit bulls. I shared a bedroom with my three brothers. Our sisters shared the other bedroom. Four guys in one room led to plenty of brawls. All Dad had to do was shoot his deadly glare, and whatever activity drew his focus was quickly terminated. Sometimes he employed other means. Our hallway measured fifteen feet in length and I remember on more than one occasion getting my ass kicked up and down it.

Sometimes I didn't even touch ground. I was airborne for the entire fifteen-foot ass-whipping!

I rarely started trouble. I only picked on longhaired greasers and druggies, leaving the fat kids and short kids for others. If one of us kids got his lunch money stolen at school and came home whining about it, we were guaranteed an ass whipping by the old man. We were raised to defend ourselves, not to let others shove us around. I'll never forget the time we had just eaten at the local drive-in and on our way home a car cut us off. Its driver then backed up and started shouting obscenities at my old man. Dad rolled the car window down and inquired as to what the problem was. All of a sudden the other car cut off our vehicle and forced us to come to a complete stop. My dad, a 300-plus-pound man, burst out of our car and charged the other automobile. With his girth and the fact that he was tattooed from head to toe, my dad was a very intimidating figure. He was also strong as an ox and possessed a hair-trigger temper. As dad charged the other driver, he was greeted with a tire iron over the forehead. Dad's head was split wide open, but that didn't stop him. He slammed the other guy's head into the hood of our car. The other driver was a large man too, but he and his tire iron were no match for my father. All of us kids were cheering as dad pummeled the guy. Dad left his victim a bloody mess. Dad always led by example. Never start trouble, but if provoked, stand your ground and kick ass.

Athletics more than academics played a major role in my life. I always did enough in school to pass my classes, not always with flying colors, but I got the job done. The way I look at it, studying never bothered me so I never bothered studying. The rule in the Bodzianowski household was that if you were active in sports, you did not need to work at odd jobs for pocket money. My parents encouraged us to participate in sports. It kept us out of trouble and gave us something to work towards. We were a big wrestling family. All of my brothers and I wrestled from an early age. Billy, who was almost four years older than I, was my role model and hero. He was a state champion wrestler. I watched his every move and prided myself on being as much like him as possible.

Quite often, Billy and I used to battle it out with gloves out in the dog kennel. I was only about ten years old when I realized I could hold my own with my big brother. I definitely had earned his respect. I used to persuade the neighborhood kids to come over and duke it out in the kennel, but it didn't take long for them to realize who was king of the hill. Billy told a few of his friends that I was willing to lace up the gloves on a moment's notice. While Billy and I would usually end up stalemated in our kennel ring, I owned his buddies' asses. Billy was awfully proud of the fact that his little brother could whip people who were much older. It seemed I had a knack for fighting.

One of my fondest memories of being king of the kennel ring occurred when my older sister Denise's new boyfriend stopped over. I did not like him from the get go. He was a cocky biker who liked to talk tough. I wanted to know if he could back up his tough facade and invited him to go a few rounds. I was not even able to work up a sweat as I pounded this poor S.O.B. all over the kennel run. He left shortly afterwards, tail between his legs. He had gained a black eye in the scuffle and lost my sister, Denise, as his girlfriend in the process. She had realized he was all smoke but no fire—a macho talker who was whipped by his girlfriend's little brother.

Growing up, I always seemed to be near the action or right in the middle of it. I was mischievous and a daredevil.

I became bored easily and liked to create my own excitement. I remember my first day at Tinley Heights grammar school. In fact, it was the very day the brand new facility opened its doors. I got into a fight with another kid over some names he called me. Punches started flying and, the next thing I remember, I was hauled into the principal's office. I was kicked out of school for the rest of the day. Can you believe that? The first day the school opened, I was sent home. Class hadn't even begun yet. I was the first kid ever kicked out of Tinley Heights grammar school, a record I'm still proud of to this day. I was kicked out of school plenty of times after that. As long as I could convince my parents that I didn't start it, and I could boast of victory, they usually let it go. Mom did grow a little tired of visiting the principal. Remember, she didn't drive, so she either got a lift from one of her friends or legged it. On those occasions that she had to walk, I definitely heard about it. My Dad's response never varied: "Craig, don't start fights, but if I ever hear you got your ass kicked, just know that you got another ass kicking coming when I get a hold of you." He meant every word he said. Fortunately, I never once had to tell my dad that I got beat up. I was always known as the toughest kid in the class. Although I never had to tell my Dad I lost a fight, it did not mean that I was exempt from one of his ass whippings. If one of us got out of line, we got smacked. Dad was very strict. You didn't even think about giving him back talk. If you even dreamed about it in your sleep, you'd best wake up and apologize to him. That was the way he was raised, and he felt it was the best way to raise his own. I respected my old man a great deal, and can honestly say that any ass whipping I got, I probably deserved. My Dad was a fair man. He was an equal opportunity ass kicker.

All of us Bodzianowski kids turned out just fine. There are no druggies or felons among us. Dad always said that if we were caught with cigarettes he would tear an arm off. Can you imagine if I ever smoked marijuana and got caught? It would have been off with my head. That alone was a good enough reason to leave drugs alone. Sure, I got into my share of mischief, but I was never a bad kid—the kind you read about so often today. Trouble between kids when I was growing up was settled with fists, not knives or guns. We did not have gangs or do drugs, but raised a little hell. . . you bet!

TWO

Donna DeBauche (sister)*: "A daredevil is the best word to describe my brother. He was always up for a challenge of any sort. Craig and I were only a year apart and we were very close. We both rode the same bus to school. One time, Craig had an M-80 firecracker and he flashed it at me as we sat near the back of the bus. I shook my head and informed him not to set it off. He just grinned. Craig lit the M-80 and dropped it behind his seat at the end of the bus. BAM! The bus driver slammed on his brakes when he heard the explosion go off. The bus came to a screeching halt as the kids jeered in amusement. Everyone but the driver knew that Craig started the fireworks. The bus driver charged out of his chair and demanded the identity of the guilty party. Nobody uttered a word. It was a cold February day and the driver threatened that we* *would all walk to and from school for the next month. Once again, there was no response. Although many kids, including us, lived several miles from school, no one dared to snitch on Craig. Nobody ever narked on a Bodzianowski. We had a reputation in the area and no one dared to get on Craig's bad side. Nobody ever squealed on Craig, and for the next month we all hoofed it back and forth to school in freezing cold weather."*

"Craig was a leader everyone respected, and no one messed with. He had proven his toughness at a young age and his reputation always preceded him."

Sure, I was a bit of a hellion, but it was basically all good clean fun. I attempted shoplifting once, but paid a heavy price for it. I was with one of my pals and we were caught stealing dog food, of all things. On a dare of course… Off to the police station we went. The cop brought us there to teach us a lesson. They called my house. Lucky for me it was in the evening and dad was working second-shift. I watched in horror as they dialed home to inform my parents about my K-Mart five-finger discount. The officer reached my mom and a discussion began. I could tell by the bizarre look on his face that it wasn't going the way he hoped. My mother informed him that her children were not thieves, and said that it must be somebody else's kid, not her Craig. Then she hung up the phone. Mom knew they had the right juvenile but it was her way of teaching me a lesson. Once again the officer telephoned and another twisted look crossed his face as the conversation with my mother continued. I could hear a dial tone in the background. Before Mom hung up again, she informed the police officer that she had no driver's license, so I would just have to wait for my dad to get off work and handle the situation.

I sat in a cell and felt my butt get sore just thinking about what would happen when Dad arrived. My partner in crime had been released hours earlier leaving me to wait out my sentence alone. Finally, Dad arrived. He shot me a cold glare upon arrival as they released me from my cell. I had been taught not to steal, and the fact that Dad would be tired after a long night's work, and upset about having to come to the police station could only make my punishment worse than any judge could hand out.

The first half of our trip back home was quiet. Dad didn't say a word. I just sat there afraid to say anything that might anger him even more. Finally, he snarled, "Craig, you know what you did was wrong, and you know what is next, right?"

"Yes," I answered, thinking that a royal ass whipping was about to commence. What happened next was a large shock.

"You no longer can take karate lessons!" Dad declared.

"Whew!" I thought to myself, "no problem. You can keep the karate lessons as long as I don't get my ass beat." Of course, I acted then as if losing my karate lessons was a major blow. I didn't want to give Dad any second thoughts concerning my punishment. That day ended any plan I may have had of making it big as a thief. I realized that although it was just a stupid dare, it was wrong and I would never do it again. Fortunately, I stayed active in sports, which left me with only a limited amount of time to raise some hell.

Contact sports, especially wrestling, were a way of life in the Bodzianowski household. As I said, Dad was a decent amateur boxer in his day. He competed in nineteen bouts and won most of them. Being married at age sixteen and cranking out kids right away dissolved any thought he had of continuing a ring career. Dad wasn't a big sports fan in general, but he loved boxing. When a fight was on the tube, we watched it. We had a punching bag hanging in the house. Boxing eventually got in my blood, but not until I tried my hand at wrestling and football.

All of my brothers wrestled at one point in their lives. I liked the one-on-one competition of wrestling, and was good at it. When I won, I could take the credit, and when I lost it was my own fault. Billy was the best wrestler in the family. He made the whole family proud the year he brought home the state championship. It made me realize how much work and dedication it takes to make it to the top. I noticed, too, the respect and adulation that came with being a champ. These were first-hand lessons I learned from my brother. I would never forget them.

Following my brother's example, I started wrestling in sixth grade with the Tinley Bulldogs and competed through most of my high school years. I also played football my freshman and sophomore years, an experience that would change my life. That's where I got a serious start in boxing. Some of my buddies on the football team were taking a twelve-week boxing class in the suburb of Palos Park. I had always been a natural with the gloves on, and I was excited when they invited me to come along to the boxing gym. The first day I walked into that boxing gym, I felt at home.

Having discovered my passion for boxing, football and all other sports and activities fell by the wayside. I had always been a good fighter, the kennel champ. The boxing ring at the gym didn't look all that different from the kennel. It was an enclosed area with nowhere to hide—just the way I liked it. My life was soon to change. I had found organized boxing, my niche in life. I also met two men at the Palos Park boxing gym that would have an enormous influence on my life as well as my boxing career. Mr. Bill O'Connor was a top amateur boxing official, and Nate Bolden was a former middleweight contender who became my coach and mentor.

THREE

I vividly remember walking into the Palos Park boxing gym for the first time. A few boxers were duking it out behind me. Fight posters and mirrors covered the walls. In the background I could hear the rat-tat-tat of the speed bag, and the thumping noise of power punches connecting with the heavy bag.

A man tapped me on the shoulder and introduced himself as Bill O'Connor. He was obviously a man of class, impeccably groomed from head-to-toe in a very professional manner. Mr. O'Connor explained to me that he had fought as an amateur and that boxing had gotten into his blood. Now he was a coach, a judge, and a referee. He also devoted lots of time to the Catholic Youth Organization (CYO) and its boxing program. We hit it off right away. Mr. O'Connor told me that if I was serious about learning how to box, I had come to the right place. Then he pointed to an elderly African-American man in the far corner of the gym and said, "That man is Nate Bolden, a former middleweight contender, who had nearly one hundred professional fights. He will serve as your coach. You're lucky to have such a well-schooled ex-fighter like Nate as your first coach. Your first coach is your most important coach, and Nate knows all the tricks of the trade. He will teach you the proper technique from the beginning. Nate is the only real old timer left in this area."

When I introduced myself, I said, "Hello, Mr. Nate Bolden, my name is Craig Bodzianowski and I want to learn how to box."

In a soft voice, he replied "Nate, call me Nate, son." Then he led me to a mirror and began teaching me the proper boxing stance and the correct way to hold my hands. When I told him I was naturally left-handed, Nate said, "Son, you may be but I will teach you how to box in the orthodox right-handed stance, and you will have a natural, strong left jab and a powerful left hook." It sounded fine to me, but it brings up a point I want to address. As my professional boxing career progressed, it was often reported that I was a converted southpaw. In fact, I may be naturally left-handed, but I never fought out of the southpaw stance. From day one, Nate trained me to fight as a righty. As my first boxing practice wound down, I couldn't wait to get home and tell my dad that our family now had a second-generation amateur boxer.

Dad was almost as excited as I was. When I told him about Nate Bolden, Dad got even more excited. "I sure know about him," he said. "He is one of the best boxers to ever come out of the Chicago area. He holds victories over former middleweight champions Tony Zale and Jake 'The Raging Bull' La Motta!" While I didn't really know many old-time fighters, I was well aware of Zale and La Motta. The former was from nearby Gary, Indiana, and was a legend in Chicago, where he had often fought. I had seen a movie about the life and times of Jake La Motta called “Raging Bull’.

“Stick with Nate Bolden,” Dad instructed. “He will teach you something.”

I worked hard at improving my boxing technique. I never missed practice, and at the gym I went all-out to master my new sport. Nate saw I had a strong punch. His goal was to make me a great technical boxer, too. But he also taught me not to turn down a knockout if it presented itself. In his day, Nate had been a scientific boxer. Now he was passing on his vast experience and wisdom to me. He really harped on developing my left jab, calling it a boxer’s most important weapon, the punch that sets up all other combinations. He taught me how to throw the jab straight out, putting my shoulder and full body weight behind it for maximum force. I worked on it relentlessly until I had it mastered. Nate knew all the defensive tricks, too, like catching punches off the shoulders and rolling with them to minimize their impact. Every day, under his eye, I learned something new.

As my junior year of high school approached, I decided to stick with boxing and retire from football. I really liked football, but the ring was my passion. I felt as if I couldn’t play football and devote a one hundred percent effort to boxing. Luckily for me, the Palos Park Gym was closer to school than it was to home. I’d head out of school at 2:20 and walk to the gym where I’d wait outside on the porch for practice to begin at 7 p.m.

As time went on, my bond with Mr. O’Connor and Nate grew strong. Mr. O’Connor was a successful salesman for a large steel company. He was a positive thinker who was always filling my mind with such thoughts as: “What the mind can conceive, the body can achieve;" and "If its to be, it's up to me." These aphorisms really hit home, and I tried to follow them in my daily life.

One day I told Mr. O'Connor that I heard Nate had fought both Tony Zale and Jake LaMotta. "Nate fought many top contenders in his day," he told me. "He fought Zale four times, winning two of those contests. Nate was the uncrowned champion. He also fought former world light-heavyweight champions, Joey Maxim and Archie Moore. Maxim had once defended his title by stopping one of boxing's all-time greats, Sugar Ray Robinson. Moore held the title for nearly ten years and was also boxing's all-time knockout king. Nate fought Moore twice, dropping close decisions both times."

Archie Moore (former light-heavyweight champion in 1997 interview): *"I fought Nate Bolden twice in my career. The first time we fought was at a small club in New York called St. Nicholas Arena. Nate was a very scientific fighter like myself. It was my first fight in New York. I defeated him on a close decision over ten rounds. I fought Nate again later on in my career in Baltimore, Maryland. Nate was ranked ahead of me at that time as a middleweight contender. I knew that if I eventually wanted to earn a shot at the title that I would have to defeat Nate to move up the rankings. Nate had made a good name for himself in Baltimore. He had scored some impressive victories there before our bout took place. Once again, I was victorious by another close ten-round decision. Nate Bolden was a great fighter who defeated several outstanding boxers in* *his career. As world-rated fighters, we had a mutual respect for each other."*

Nate was something special. He was a humble man who left the bragging to others. I could tell how much Nate enjoyed teaching young kids to box. He had a way of making all of his boxers feel wanted, even the ones who didn't have a lot of potential. Nate coached kids from the street or from the suburbs, it didn't matter to him. He was someone you could look up to. Nate cared.

Mr. O'Connor also informed me that Jake La Motta had mentioned Nate in his autobiography, "Raging Bull", on which the hit movie was based. He recommended I go to the library and check it out. "That's just what I'll do," I claimed, at the same time wondering to myself where the hell the library was located.

Once I found the library, I stormed the shelves in search of *Raging Bull.* As soon as I found the book, I dove into it, searching for words about my coach, Nate Bolden. I soon found the part where La Motta described his battle with Nate:

> "What's funny was that I got some of my biggest notices over a fight that I lost with a guy named Nate Bolden at Marigold Gardens in Chicago. And, when I say I *lost* I mean I got *beat*! Jesus Christ, what a pounding! If he'd been stronger he'd have flattened me. I've granted right from the beginning that I never was the world's greatest classic boxer. What gave me the most trouble with Bolden was that he was a straight boxer. He wanted absolutely nothing but points. A guy like Sugar Ray Robinson, for example, he was a real 'cutie' when it came to boxing, but he also

> liked the knockout on his record, so there came a point in the fight where he figured to take a few on the chance of getting a knockout. Bolden had no intention of mixing it up at all. What he intended to do—and what he did do—was to let me charge, let me swing, and all he did was jab, dance, counter punch, duck, hit.
>
> "Like I said, I lost, and not only did I lose but he hit me so much that I was as much a mess as I've ever been. Those sliding punches of his weren't intended to knock me out because he knew he couldn't. That Bolden is one of those wise guys, jab, jab, jab. A couple more rounds and I would have had him!"

To read these paragraphs written by Jake "The Raging Bull" La Motta about my coach seemed unbelievable. Everyone in boxing knew Jake La Motta, and here was the former world champion, a boxing legend, talking about how Nate kicked his ass. Most amazing to me was that La Motta, one of boxing's most famous tough guys, openly admitted that Nate should have knocked him out. It was hard to believe Jake La Motta acknowledged such a thing but he did. Read the book!

I was thrilled to have such a highly regarded and accomplished fighter as Nate for a mentor. I wondered why he never received a shot at a world title. His credentials surely seemed to merit it. When I brought this up with Mr. O'Connor, he said, "Craig, Nate never had the proper backing, the proper connections, the proper management. There were several other tremendous boxers that never got what they deserved. One of the greatest fighters of all time, Charley Burley, never even received a title shot, and Archie Moore had to wait almost seventeen years for his first crack at a world title!"

Archie Moore (1997 interview): *"Guys like Nate and I were at a disadvantage in the fight game. On some fight cards, black fighters could only get on the show by fighting each other. Sometimes guys like Nate or me would be offered money to throw a fight to the local favorite. I had to wait almost seventeen years for my first title shot. I wasn't going to lie down for anybody and neither was Nate. That's one reason why Nate may have never gotten a chance to fight for a world title."*

Nate had my total respect. I worked hard to learn as much about boxing from him as possible. I was anxious for my first sanctioned amateur bout. I was in good physical condition, and I wanted to apply my newly learned skills in an actual contest. I had been pounding the piss out of other kids in the gym. Nate said he would get me a fight on the next local amateur show.

The next time I showed up at the gym, Nate informed me that my first amateur fight would be in a week I knew I was ready and quite capable of handling myself. Hadn't I always faired well in all my unsanctioned competitions?

I arrived at the arena for my first bout accompanied by Nate, Mr. O'Connor, and my mom. Throughout my fight career, Mom hardly ever missed a fight. Sometimes Dad would be out of town with the pit bulls, but when he was there for a fight I think he had a tougher time watching me than Mom did.

Butterflies danced in my stomach as I searched the weigh-in for potential opponents. Nate came over and pointed out my opponent. "Craig, you will be fighting that kid seated over there with the long hair."

"Yes!" I exclaimed aloud as I remembered the longhaired kids I'd pounded on in school. That was just a little added incentive to pummel this hippie.

Mom came over and said, "Craig, just go out and kick his ass!" She was always known for giving her children good wholesome advice!

I took Mom's advice to heart and went out and annihilated this poor fellow. I starched him in the opening round. The bell rang and I just charged out throwing haymakers until the referee stopped the fight. It felt good to get my first win under my belt and I was thirsty for more competition.

After only a couple of months, I had scored a few more impressive victories. Nate was happy with my progress so far, and felt I needed a test against a more experienced boxer to find out just how far I had advanced. Nate worked out an arrangement for me to box Don Lee of Gary, Indiana. I had never heard of him, but Nate knew all about the boxer nicknamed "Dangerous Don." Nate told me Lee was a southpaw who would switch from fighting conventional to left-handed during the course of a bout. Lee was one of the finest amateurs in the country, he said, and win or lose, it would be a vital learning experience. I never worried about who my opponent was. That was Nate's job. If he felt I was ready to fight a guy like Lee, that was all that I needed to hear.

The fight took place in a small gymnasium in Worth, Illinois. From the opening bell, I decided to take the fight right to Lee. He came out in the conventional right-handed stance. I pressured him all through the first round, taking a few good shots but answering back with some of my own.

When the bell sounded, I walked confidently back to my corner. Nate told me that I won the opening session and should keep pressuring Lee. Unfortunately for me, Lee decided to alter his strategy in round two, and came out boxing as a southpaw. It confused me. He never hurt me over the next two rounds, but managed to out-box me and was awarded the decision. I was just starting to solve his style but the bell sounded to end the third and final round before I could land a finishing blow and knock out Lee. Who knows? Maybe if I had a few more rounds… That was one of the problems with amateur boxing. All bouts are scheduled for only three rounds. Sometimes I needed a few extra rounds to land a finishing knockout punch.

> **Don Lee (former world ranked professional middleweight contender)**: *"Craig was a tough, aggressive fighter the night we fought. Craig gave me a lot of trouble early in the fight. Whenever I got into trouble, I switched to southpaw, and in this fight it definitely helped. I went on to win the 1979 National Golden Gloves title."*

I was disappointed after the decision was announced in Lee's favor. It was the first time that I had lost a fight, in or out of the ring. Nate said to use it as a learning experience and that back in the gym we would work on my mistakes. I did improve as a result of my loss, and Lee did pretty well himself. He went on to a successful professional career. He cracked the top ten ratings in the middleweight division. I remember watching him knockout the British champion, Tony Sibson, on national television. Don's first nineteen victories in the paid ranks came by knockout. He had a hell of a punch, but he never knocked out Craig Bodzianowski. Nobody did!

I wasted no time getting back to the gym. I begged Nate daily to get me another fight as soon as possible. At the same time, my high school wrestling coach asked me to re-join the wrestling team. The sectional wrestling meet was approaching and my school needed an established wrestler to compete at 175 pounds. The Golden Gloves tournament was also approaching. I was supposed to fight at 165 pounds. I didn't feel like gaining and then losing a bunch of weight. Boxing was where my heart was, so I'd give my body to it, too.

I started to make a name for myself in the local amateur ranks. I scored a couple knockout victories and was ready for the Chicago Park District tournament. I won my first few bouts in the tournament and advanced to the championship. I'll never forget that night of my first amateur title match. It was a school night and I had an important homework assignment due the next day. I knew my bout would be one of the last matches of the night, so I found a quiet corner of the arena and buried my head in my biology book. Suddenly I was interrupted by two kids. "Hey, are you Bodzianowski?" they inquired.

"Yep, that's me," I replied without looking up.

"You're fighting Antonio and he is going to knock you out!" they jeered. I picked up my book and stormed off. Nate noticed my anger and tried to calm me down, explaining the importance of boxing with a clear head. He had been a thinking man's fighter himself, and he trained me the same way.

Nate had studied my opponent throughout the entire tournament and he knew what I needed to do. "Craig, go to the body, he's a taller opponent," he said. "Get inside on him and break him in half." Nate was on the button when it came to knowing an opponent's weakness and laying out a game plan. On this night, however, I almost ended up sorry it worked.

As I entered the ring for the 165-pound championship match, I could feel the usual butterflies dancing in my stomach. I was still angry from the taunts of Antonio's fan club. I glared across the ring, and Antonio returned a cocky stare. Nate slipped in my mouthpiece and mumbled for the millionth time that evening, "Body, body, go to the body."

I charged out of my corner at the bell. I slipped Antonio's jab, moved inside and I began working over his mid-section with some vicious body punches. As I kept landing with straight right hands and left hooks to the body, I could see Antonio's hands lowering to protect his gut. When the bell sounded, Antonio looked like a beaten fighter.

"He's yours son! Keep throwing body punches," Nate advised between rounds. I jumped back on the offensive when the second round began, resuming my body attack. I dug deep with a left uppercut that found its mark right on Antonio's solar plexus. It knocked the wind right out of him, but that wasn't the only thing that came out of him. He horked all over me! The referee raised my hand in victory but I was only interested in getting into the shower as fast as possible. I got no hugs of congratulations immediately following this victory!

I moved up to the 178 pound-class and claimed another tournament victory in a Catholic Youth Organization meet. But it was a bittersweet victory.

Ten days before the tournament, my brother Billy was shot in a freak accident at our home. Billy had been back from the Marines less than a month. We were all relaxing at home watching the Chicago Bears. Billy was with his girlfriend in the dining room showing her the family gun collection. His girlfriend handled one of the guns and said how much she had always wanted one. Billy told her to put the gun down. It was loaded. Somehow the revolver went off, killing my brother. It seemed so unreal. It was a senseless mistake. The loss haunted my family. I lost the man I had patterned myself after. There was no more brother here to follow. Understanding my loss, Mr. O'Connor convinced me to compete in the tournament as scheduled. I went out and won for my brother. I think of Billy often, but discussing his life pains me to this day.

The boxing gym at Palos Park was closing its doors early in 1979. Fortunately for me, Nate also trained fighters at a south side gym called the Woodlawn Boys Club. It was in the worst neighborhood in Chicago. If you saw a cat wandering around and it still had its tail, you knew it hadn't been there long. The whole area surrounding the Woodlawn Boys Club seemed hopeless. It was as if a black cloud hung over the place. On one side of the gym there was an abandoned movie theater. On the other side was an empty lot littered with broken glass and the remains of uninhabited homes. Above the gym, "The El," an elevated train, creaked by every fifteen minutes. It was a different world than the friendly surroundings of Palos Park. However, this was Nate's gym, and everyone there had the highest respect for him. It was home to many experienced professional fighters, whereas Palos Park was just a small amateur club in the suburbs. I liked my new surroundings, at least on the inside. The gym had two large elevated rings, an assortment of heavy bags, and a big weight room. I could see the opportunity to learn more and advance my boxing career here.

It may have seemed like a white kid from the suburbs had no business in a tough inner-city gym like Woodlawn Boys Club, but I was always treated with the utmost respect. I earned it by climbing into the ring with the top professional boxers there. The locals realized that this Polish kid could fight. In all the years that I trained there, I only had one altercation and that was outside the gym.

I usually arrived to work out in mid-afternoon and always parked my truck on the street as close to the gym as possible. Two bums hung out on the corner, and daily hit me up for spare change. I was happy to oblige, and in exchange they agreed to keep an eye on my vehicle. It seemed like a fair enough deal to me. One day, however, I arrived a few hours later than usual. It was dark out and the two old guys were nowhere to be found. Two young street thugs approached me as I got out of my truck. "Got any spare change?" they asked.

"Nope," I replied. I attempted to walk around them to avoid conflict. Suddenly, one of the hoodlums tried to reach in my pocket for my wallet! Instinct took over. I blasted him with a right hand that smashed his nose. He fell hard, and the other punk took off running as I sprinted to the entrance of the gym. In that depressed area anything could happen. It was the knives, guns, and gang violence that I wanted no part of. I was there to box.

One of the toughest fighters to ever come out of Chicago was Alfonzo Ratliff. Eventually he would become a world champion, but when I began to frequent Woodlawn, Ratliff's professional career was just getting started. He was the hottest prospect in the gym and I sparred with him on several occasions. Soon I would be entering my first Golden Gloves tournament, and knew that all the work I could get with this highly touted prospect would improve me as a boxer. Ratliff used to pummel his sparring partners so hard that a lot of them would quit right in the middle of a round. Even though I was still just an amateur, I was proud of the fact that I could hold my own with Ratliff in the ring. I could tell it wouldn't be long before he reached the top. What I didn't know then was that Ratliff and I would eventually meet again in two grueling professional encounters.

Another one of my early Woodlawn sparring partners was a guy named Oliver McCall. He went on to win the world heavyweight championship in1994 by knocking out Lennox Lewis in London and to date is the only man to ever defeat Lewis. We used to engage in some heated sparring sessions at Woodlawn. McCall mostly trained at a south side gym named Fuller Park, just a stone's throw from Comiskey Park. McCall had difficulty finding sparring partners, so he used to come over to Woodlawn to get ring work. McCall threw nothing but power punches. This is where being a well-schooled defensive boxer paid off. I used to catch McCall's blows on my gloves or shoulders, but I could feel the strength behind those bombs. Oliver used to knock out guys in the gym. McCall served as a sparring partner for Mike Tyson for a few years, and he was one of the few guys who could actually hold his own with Tyson in the gym. I've heard he has embarked on the comeback trail after battling drug and psychological problems. I wish him the best.

It was in high school while training to be a boxer that I got my name. Carl Sandburg High School had its share of preppy kids from the surrounding suburbs. At that time Izod shirts were the "in" thing with that set. They were a pricey item, a bit beyond my limited budget. One thing I could afford was a tattoo, courtesy of the old man. I came up with the idea of getting him to tattoo the Izod trademark alligator over my left breast. He did a terrific job, and you couldn't beat the price. I cut holes in all my shirts to expose my alligator tattoo. I was the ultimate preppie! Kids started calling me "Gator". I've answered to it ever since.

FOUR

Graduation came in June of 1979. I was proud to earn my diploma. At that time I didn't even consider professional boxing as a post-graduate career. I was already managing a gas station and getting ready to compete in the Golden Gloves tournament.

I had been maintaining my rigorous training regime at Woodlawn and sometimes also worked out at the Riverdale Boxing Club. Although Riverdale had plenty of talented amateur fighters, Woodlawn was best for me because it had the top professionals. From them I could learn the most. Nate had worked out an arrangement to train boxers three times a week at Riverdale, and wherever Nate went I followed. We rotated sessions between the two clubs. At Riverdale I hooked up with an old acquaintance of mine named Pat Guilfoyle. Pat was Irish, full of piss and vinegar. He liked to fight outside of the ring almost as much as I did. Guilfoyle was the kind of guy who would fight anyone at the drop of a hat. We had met back in grade school and had almost come to blows right away. It was the summer after sixth grade, and my brother Howard and I had gone to neighboring Tinley Park for a day of swimming. You could swim all day at the high school for a buck. We rode our bikes to the pool and were hassled as we attempted to lock them to a bike rack. A local punk noticed a tattoo on my arm and he said, "You think you're pretty tough with that tattoo, huh?" I admitted as much, and the punk said, "Well, you wouldn't stand a chance against either of the Guilfoyle brothers."

"Bring 'em on!" I confidently fired back. Later that day, Howard and I were confronted in the locker room by Pat and his brother Mike. A few insults were exchanged, but luckily for the Guilfoyle brothers, no punches were thrown. A few years later, Pat and I became close friends, and we've raised plenty of hell since then. Though Pat was a lot smaller than me, pound-for-pound Pat was one of the baddest roughnecks around. The S.O.B. was tougher than a four-dollar steak.

One night after training at Riverdale, Pat and I decided to go to the drive-in with a few buddies. The feature movie that evening was a low-budget monster flick. It didn't take long before we got bored and restless. Somebody else who didn't like bad monster movies tried to bet us that we couldn't climb down the front of the big screen. At first we declined, but once the wager reached $150, it was a go. That's a lot of cash when you consider that most guys our age were making three bucks an hour flipping burgers.

Pat and I climbed up the back of the movie screen. We tied a long rope to the top and dropped it down the front. As the feature presentation kept rolling, we began our descent. We were about ten feet from the ground when the movie suddenly stopped and the drive-in lights came on. At that point our only option was to jump the remaining distance and haul ass into a nearby cornfield. The authorities were on their way. Luckily, the corn was high and the "on-screen" bad guys made a safe getaway.

Pat started boxing several years before me. At Riverdale he frequently sparred with professional lightweight contender, Johnny Lira. Lira had once challenged for the world 135-pound title, losing to champion, Ernesto Espana, in a bout staged in Chicago. Pat spent several months working out with Lira for his world title attempt and in the process improved tremendously as a fighter.

Johnny Lira had quite a story on his own. He went undefeated in his first eighteen professional bouts, capturing the American lightweight title along the way. But it almost didn't happen. Lira ran with a tough crowd as a youth and once took a bullet in the leg from a rival gang leader. The wound became badly infected and the doctors recommended amputation. Lira had friends sneak him a fifth of vodka and a pair of crutches in the hospital. Properly anesthetized, Lira escaped in the middle of the night. Whenever the pain returned, he doused his leg with vodka. After a few weeks on the run, Lira returned to the hospital and the doctors did not amputate. His leg improved. Johnny said at the time that he knew his hopes for a boxing career would have vanished with the loss of a leg. Who knew that I would end up disproving that notion?

I planned to make a name for myself in the 1980 Golden Gloves tournament. But there was a big potential stumbling block. My competition in the 178-pound class would include LeeRoy Murphy, who'd won the National Golden Gloves championship the year before. As soon as it was announced that he would be entering the Chicago Golden Gloves tournament a lot of other contestants dropped out. Murphy had just knocked out the Russian champion in Moscow.

My friend Pat was the 139-pound favorite. He and I cruised through our first couple tournament bouts at St. Andrew's Gym, located just a few blocks from ivy-covered Wrigley Field.

When I arrived for the semi-finals, the first thing I did was check the pairings for that night. The board read "178-pound Craig Bodzianowski vs. LeeRoy Murphy." The moment of truth had arrived. I knew our meeting was inevitable, and I had prepared myself mentally for the task.

I went to the locker room, changed, and then found Nate. He gave me the usual pre-fight pep talk and I loosened up. As I stretched and began to wrap my hands, I watched the lighter weight division fights. Pat scored a unanimous decision victory to advance to the finals the following week at the International Amphitheater. Now it was my turn.

Murphy and I traded bombs for almost three rounds. He was a well-polished boxer with dynamite in either hand. I felt more than one of his powerful punches connect with my sturdy chin. I hung in with Murphy toe-to-toe. Before the third round, Nate told me it was a close fight and I needed to win the final round in order to seal the victory. Once again, Murphy and I went punch-for-punch for most of the round. He caught me with a decent one near the end of the round, and all of a sudden the referee jumped in and stopped the fight. People were booing, and cups and debris were hurled into the ring. I felt I had been robbed. Murphy had never put me down or even staggered me. He landed plenty of power punches, but I had returned my share of hard shots. That the fight had been stopped was beyond belief. Apparently the audience agreed, for I received a thunderous ovation as I returned to the locker room.

Pat went on to win the Golden Gloves title the following week by decisioning Sam Lucas. As I saw Pat's hand raised in victory, I made a silent vow that nothing would stop me from winning next year's tournament. It was of some consolation to me when Murphy went on to be captain of the United States boxing team in the 1980 Olympics. Unfortunately for him, President Jimmy Carter boycotted the Olympics that year and killed any hopes he had for a gold medal.

> **LeeRoy Murphy: (former IBF world cruiserweight champion)** *"I had won the last five Chicago Golden Gloves tournaments in my weight class. Some people felt that Craig would prevent me from winning my sixth title. I had over 350 amateur bouts and this would be my final Golden Gloves tournament.*
>
> *"The first round of my fight with Craig was real close. Craig came out swinging right from the opening bell. Craig hit me with everything in the first round. My corner instructed me to go after him in the second round. We went to war. I stayed on the offensive until they stopped the fight.*
>
> *"Craig and I eventually became friends. Craig was always fun to have around. He is one of those guys that can keep you laughing all day long."*

My goal for 1981 was to be the Chicago Golden Gloves champion. I knew it would require plenty of hard work, but I was willing to make the sacrifice. Unfortunately, my pal Pat would not be around. Pat represented the United States in a meet against the Ireland national team. After that, Pat enlisted in the Marine Corps and was off to boot camp. I would miss my hell-raising buddy!

I was now working out exclusively at the Woodlawn Boys Club. Nate was pushing me harder than ever. He had me punching the heavy bag until I could literally punch no more. Every morning, at a field by his house near the University of Chicago, Nate would have me run, then sprint, then run, then sprint again. He was a strong believer in interval training to increase cardiovascular capacity. Nate could make one mile feel like seven. He always told us that this was what he did in his professional days, and it would suit us too. It did. I was knocking guys around the gym like never before.

I was also putting on muscle, and was forced to move up to the heavyweight division. One of my first bouts of 1981 was against the nation's fifth-ranked heavyweight, Michael Brothers. Nate felt that I was ready for the challenge. I couldn't wait to prove him right. Before the match, Nate instructed me to stay busy. Brothers was a classic boxer, and to win I would need to get inside his jab and work the body. I followed Nate's orders, constantly slipping Brothers' jab and working in close. I banged the hell out of his body and then attacked his head. My hand was raised in victory. I had successfully made the adjustment to the heavyweight ranks and was now one of the favorites to win the 1981 Golden Gloves heavyweight championship.

Again the preliminary bouts were held at St. Andrew's gym. I was in the best shape of my career. At times it was difficult knowing my buddies were out nightly, raising hell, while I stayed in and tended to the business at hand. Getting proper rest and monitoring my food intake were necessary to reach peak fighting form. The sacrifice paid off as I won all three of my preliminary bouts and advanced to the finals. The finals would be held at the brand new Rosemont Horizon, home of the then collegiate basketball powerhouse, DePaul Blue Demons.

My opponent turned out to be an old acquaintance, Jim Finn. Finn had once been trained by Nate, and we had sparred several times. It had always been give-and-take warfare, and I expected no less in our championship encounter. On the program we were both listed as boxing out of Woodlawn, but Nate would work my corner that night. There would be eleven championship bouts before Finn and I would square off in the evening's finale. I'd be lucky if Finn and I were swapping punches by midnight.

Almost 9,000 fans were on hand to witness the 54th Chicago Golden Gloves finals. It was a showcase for the city's top amateur stars. I remained loose and self-assured as I watched bits and pieces of each bout before mine. Randy Smith squeaked out a close decision over Allen "The Mule Man" Alexander at 165 pounds to capture his fifth consecutive Golden Gloves title. One of the biggest disappointments of the evening occurred when nationally-ranked 125 pound Charlie "White Lightning" Brown won by default, because his scheduled opponent incurred an eye injury just a few days before the finals. "White Lightning" was one crazy S.O.B. He had a reputation for partying all night before a fight, but somehow always managed to win. Knowing that Charlie Brown had qualified to represent Chicago against the New York Champions was an added incentive for victory. Life was never dull when Charlie "White Lightning" Brown was around.

When it was my turn in the ring, Finn attempted to psyche me out by giving me his best tough guy look. I couldn't wait to knock it off his smug face. The bell rang and I charged out of my corner. We met in center ring and went toe-to-toe for the entire three rounds. It was phone booth warfare at its finest. I landed several powerful shots on Finn's granite jaw. He returned almost as many punches as he received. Finn lacked the necessary defensive skills to thwart my attack. On the other hand, I was able to block or slip many of his potent punches. At the end of the second round, Nate warned me that it was extremely close and said I needed to win the third to ensure a victory. Finn and I continued to trade bombs in the final round. When the bell sounded to end the fight, I knew it was a squeaker but I felt I did enough to win. I circled the ring like a caged lion waiting for the decision to be announced. Those few minutes seemed like hours. At last the announcer grabbed the microphone and declared that it was a split-decision. The large crowd was suddenly silent as the announcer then proclaimed, "The winner and 1981 Chicago Golden Gloves Heavyweight Champion .... Craig Bodzianowski!" Wow, did that ever have a nice ring to it! All the hard work paid off. It was a great feeling. Almost every living person I knew witnessed my victory. Nate and Mr. O'Connor were very proud. Mom especially enjoyed the tournament.

Next up was the national tournament in Toledo, Ohio, followed by the dual meet in New York. Needless to say, competing in the 1981 National Golden Gloves Tournament was quite an honor, although it turned out to be a major disappointment. The nation's top amateur boxers were all there. The Chicago champions took a bus to Toledo.

During the ride I rehashed my strategy over in my mind. The fights were held at the Toledo Sports Arena. Three rings were to be used simultaneously during the first three nights of the tournament. There were ninety-two bouts scheduled the opening night, and my opponent was Joe Gill of Omaha, Nebraska. I had never heard of Gill before, and never heard much of him afterwards. He wasn't much of a fighter, and would have made a terrible offensive lineman to boot, because holding was all he knew.

Gill held on to me all three rounds. Each time I tried to fire off a combination, he'd grab and hold. He would throw a punch and then tie me up. When the bell ended the frustrating contest, I threw my hands up in the air as a sign of victory. Somehow the judges saw it differently and awarded Gill the decision. Even Gill seemed surprised by the gift. The tournament was quite a let down. I figured that I had a decent shot at winning the national title, but now that dream had been choked off in a wrestling match.

It was a disappointing tournament for our entire team. We did not have a national champion among us that year. I remember returning back to our hotel after the fights and hearing that someone attempted to assassinate Pope John Paul II. A Turkish terrorist had shot him in the stomach, arm, and hand. Why someone would want to injure such a holy man made no sense to me. At the time I had no idea that in a few years I would actually be seated in the Vatican at the altar with the Pope. In my eyes, he was second in command from the top, behind only the Almighty. Whenever I think back to the national tournament in Toledo, thoughts of the Pope always come to mind.

I was becoming burnt out with amateur boxing. It had been a busy year, and I still had the match in New York against the New York Golden Gloves champion. The New York team included some of the nation's top amateurs. Mark Breland, their welterweight, was regarded as the nation's best in that class. This was his fifth consecutive year representing New York in the intra-city meet. My opponent was highly touted Carl "The Truth" Williams. At 6'5", Williams towered over most of his opponents, including me. He had just won the championship at the 1981 World Games in the Philippines, and was expected to turn professional after our match.

We had some shooters of our own. Randy Smith, our 165-pounder, had won five straight Chicago Golden Gloves titles, and lost in the finals of the 1980 Olympic trials. He was smooth as silk in the ring and almost equally as smooth outside the ring with the ladies. I think he was more excited about chasing the women in New York than fighting at Madison Square Garden. Another exceptional fighter on our team was Charlie "White Lightning" Brown. He was a hyper S.O.B. who would rather party than train, but somehow he always managed to win. He had competed in over 300 amateur fights, and had three impressive victories over future world champ Michael "Second To" Nunn.

The plane ride out to New York went fine. Throughout the flight I concentrated on the battle at hand. I thought about last year's Golden Gloves tournament and how I finished runner-up at 178 pounds. I was so glad that I moved up to heavyweight. I could now eat anything I wanted, where as the rest of my teammates had to make a certain weight limit. When meals were served, most of the guys had to skip dinner and were even spitting in cups to reduce their body weight. I enjoyed offering my starving teammates a bite of my food knowing they had to say no. I'm sure I got a better laugh out of it than they did, but at least it broke the tension a bit.

New York was the largest city I had ever visited. We stayed at the downtown Sheraton Hotel a few blocks from Times Square. Once at the hotel, I could not wait to check out the Big Apple. As soon as we unpacked, a few of us set out to see the sights. We had a day to ourselves before the fights. I remember we found a tremendous three-story arcade. It kept us busy for hours. I spent most of my money there, but it was a blast. Then we walked over to check out the legendary Madison Square Garden, where the tournament would be held. After that we hit a few other tourist traps to kill time before heading back to our hotel.

The night before a fight is usually spent relaxing in one form or another. Personally, I always liked to play cards to get my mind off of the coming fight, so I invited a few of my teammates down to my room for a game of cards. My old man loved to play poker and I learned a few tricks from him. I was on a winning streak when all of a sudden Charlie "White Lightning" Brown wandered in to rain on our poker game. He could never sit still, and in only a few minutes he managed to piss off everyone in my room, which happened to be located on the 16th floor. I demanded that Charlie get the hell out. He just laughed and then spotted a hunting knife of mine near the bed. I kept it on me at all times. My dad always had a knife attached to his belt loop, so to me it made good sense. For the most part I used it to only peel an apple or cut up whatever, and luckily that's all I ever needed it for. Charlie grabbed my knife and started jumping all around the room yelling, "Come on you big heavyweight, come get your knife!" I never knew if he was joking or not, so I just ignored him. But when he started flicking the knife near my face, I got mad. The next day I was fighting the top-ranked heavyweight in the nation, and I was in no mood for games. "Try that again and next time I'm throwing your ass out the window!" I said. Sure enough, Charlie shoved the knife in my face again. I lunged at Charlie's legs and wrestled him to the ground. I grabbed him by the ankles pushed open my window and then dangled Charlie outside by his ankles. I guess you could say that Charlie got a different view of New York City than the rest of us. Luckily, he only weighed 125 pounds so I had no problem holding on to him as he hovered above the busy streets of New York for several minutes. He begged and pleaded that he would leave us alone if I would spare his life, so I pulled him back. But then Charlie grabbed my knife again and started dancing around yelling, "Come on you big heavyweight!" I could not believe this crazy S.O.B.! This time, instead of chucking him out of the window, I stormed out of the room. In my rage of anger I might have forgotten to keep hold of him.

The weigh-ins were held the morning of the competition at Madison Square Garden. The rules stated that I still had to weigh in although my only real qualification was that I had to weigh more than 178 pounds. The morning of the fight I weighed in at slightly over 200 pounds, and then watched closely as Carl "The Truth" Williams climbed on the scale. He had an obvious advantage in height and reach, and word was that he knocked everyone out. I had never been knocked out or even knocked down, and intended to keep it that way. Williams acted extremely cocky and arrogant at the weigh-in. From the beginning, I didn't like him and I couldn't wait to give "The Truth" some honesty of my own.

Heavyweights are always the last ones to fight. To kill time, I alternately relaxed in the locker room and paced around watching the lighter weight bouts. It was another disappointing night for the Chicago team. The only fighters that had won were Randy Smith and Charlie Brown.

Brown had the potential to be one of the greatest fighters of all time. Unfortunately, he never wanted to make the sacrifices required to be the best. Charlie turned professional right after we returned from New York. His first twenty-two fights were victories, and many of those were featured on television. Brown even won a fight on the undercard of the closed circuit broadcast of the 160-pound title fight between Marvin Hagler and Roberto Duran, defeating contender, Frank Newton. "White Lightning" eventually challenged for the world lightweight title, but he lost by knockout to champion, Harry Arroyo. I heard he was up late the night before his title shot eating junk food. I didn't say Charlie "White Lightning" Brown was smart, just extremely talented. He never again contended for the title. Unlike Brown, I was lucky, for what I lacked in talent I overcame with hard work. Throughout the boxing world you hear many stories about potential championship guys who squander their talents. Not me. I made a personal promise to myself to always give one hundred percent to anything I did.

After waiting around for the preliminary fights to finish, it was finally time for the heavyweights. I was the first to enter the Garden ring to a reception of light clapping and a few boos. The crowd exploded with applause as local favorite Williams followed. At that point I really wished Nate was there with me. Nate always knew exactly the right instructions to give me before each bout and how to get me mentally focused for battle. But only two appointed coaches were allowed to join us on the trip from Chicago.

I paced uneasily, waiting for the bell. I had no formal fight plan prepared. Nate's fight strategies were the only ones I trusted, so this time I would improvise. Williams had all the obvious physical advantages, so my impromptu plan was to apply constant pressure on him and stay inside to nullify his reach advantage.

The bell sounded and Williams came out jabbing and moving, repeatedly snapping my head back with stinging lefts. As I charged forward, Williams kept popping me with hard crisp jabs. I ate a lot of leather in that opening round and came away somewhat frustrated. I could feel a welt forming under my left eye. Williams was as good as advertised and when I returned to my corner between rounds, I looked to my appointed cornermen for advice. I might as well have asked Williams himself.

"Do you want us to stop the fight?" they asked.

"What? Stop the fight! Are you crazy?" I snapped back. As I sat on my stool I tried to imagine what Nate would say. I could hear his voice in my mind, saying, "Craig, you must slip his jab and follow with a counter punch, or block the jab and then return a punch. You must prevent him from catching you flush with his left jab."

The final two rounds were very competitive as I slipped, blocked, and countered most of Williams' punches. When the bell ended the fight, I feared the opening round had cost me the decision. I wasn't surprised when Williams' hand was raised in victory. We shook hands and traded our fight jerseys; it was a ritual that had always been performed between the Chicago and New York Golden Gloves teams throughout the years.

Carl "The Truth" Williams was a hell of a talented boxer. It was obvious that he was destined to be a successful professional fighter. I remember a few years later, watching on national television as Williams challenged Larry Holmes for the world heavyweight title. Holmes got a gift decision from the judges to keep his belt. For the entire 15 rounds, Williams nailed Holmes with snapping left jabs that eventually closed Larry's left eye. On that night, Carl "The Truth" Williams should have been crowned the new world heavyweight champion.

Williams was my final amateur opponent. At the time, I really thought it was the last fight of my career. The Olympic trials were another three years down the road, and I knew my aggressive brawling style did not appeal to amateur officials. It was time for a change. I was burnt out with boxing. I was proud to retire with an amateur ring record of 62-5.

On the flight home, I realized that I was disgruntled with my construction job too, and in need of a change. The money was decent, but to do that for a living for the rest of my life felt like a death sentence. New York had been fun, and I wanted to add more adventure to my life. I had had a unique job offer presented to me before I left for New York, and it now seemed like the perfect time for a drastic lifestyle change.

FIVE

A friend of mine had approached me on the possibility of moving to Alaska. It was an idea from left field, but it had a lot going for it. I was an avid hunter and fisherman, and I couldn't think of a better place to be to pursue those interests. On the other hand, I knew there were a hell of a lot more guys than girls in Alaska, and frankly, that statistic alarmed me more than just a little. The job offer was to be a bulldozer operator, and despite the lack of girls, as soon as I returned from New York I made up my mind to go.

The day I got back I filled Nate in on my fight with Williams. He seemed proud of my effort. Nate had done a great deal for me and I was grateful. We had developed a close bond, and I could see the disappointment on his face when I told him about Alaska. "Son," he said, "you're one of my champions and you are always welcome back here. Keep in touch, my friend, I wish you the best." Nate realized I needed a change. As I walked away I knew I was really going to miss that old-timer. Still, I'd always know where to find him... at the gym training some more Golden Gloves hopefuls.

It was not surprising that it was Mr. O'Connor's nephew, Gary Shicora, who had lined up the job driving a bulldozer in Fairbanks, Alaska. Gary would even put me up rent-free until I found my own place. It was Mr. O'Connor I was going to miss more than anyone else. He had become one of my best friends. He was a true friend and helped many. Mr. O'Connor seemed to know everyone in Chicago and he used his contacts often to help a friend in need. In fact, when Nate had retired from professional prize fighting, Mr. O'Connor lined him up with a decent paying job with the City of Chicago Sanitation Department, where Nate eventually became a foreman.

Before I left, Mr. O'Connor asked if I ever gave any thought to professional boxing. "Your style of fighting is suited for the professional ranks, and I can set you up with an experienced boxing manager who would handle all the business affairs for you," he suggested.

"Thanks, Mr. O'Connor, but right now I just need to get the hell out of town," I replied. Until that very moment I had never considered fighting professionally. I now put the thought on the back burner and prepared for my long road trip.

My old man did not share my enthusiasm about the move. He just shrugged and said, "I don't understand why you have to move all the way to Alaska," and then left the room. That was sort of a stunner; I thought he would be proud of me.

My mom explained, "Craig, your father is really just mad at himself, because being that we married so young, he never had the opportunity to go on such an exciting adventure. He's really going to miss you, but he just has difficulty putting that in words." I was going to miss him too, but I told him I would be back someday. I just didn't know when.

The next day I took off for Fairbanks. Talk about a long road trip! I used to think going from one end of Chicago to the other was far. The trip took almost four days. Alaskan scenery was beautiful and I was excited about my new surroundings.

Fairbanks was a military town. The ratio of men to women was 7-to-1. Back home I always had a girlfriend or two and a few phone numbers in reserve in case of an emergency. I loved women, and meeting them in Alaska seemed like a real challenge. I had the feeling my only mode of transportation, a peddle bike, was not going to help the situation.

Fairbanks and Chicago were like night and day. In fact, when I arrived in town that's all there was—daylight. I guess there were times in the year when the days were filled with total darkness, but for now it was pure sunlight. It was pretty awesome driving around town and seeing a moose or a bear wandering around, a different kind of wildlife than I was used to seeing on Chicago streets. For an avid outdoorsman, there was no better place to be, and the fishing was awesome.

The first few weeks in Alaska were quite enjoyable. Every day was filled with new adventures. I spent long hours driving a bulldozer, and while the money was good, one thing it didn't provide was a cardiovascular workout. After a few weeks on the job my midsection began to feel a bit soft. I complained to Gary about the lack of physical work and he suggested I spend some time at the local boxing gym. As soon as I received directions to the Fort Waynewright gym, I peddled off for a workout.

It was a decent facility, but the local talent didn't compare to those back home. I remember casually walking in that first day and introducing myself. Immediately, the coach rubbed me the wrong way. During my initial workout on the heavybag he butted in with unsolicited advice, "You're throwing your left jab all wrong. Just throw it out there quick, with much less body behind it," he said.

"Whatever," I replied, continuing to punch the way Nate had taught me. I was shaking the bag with crisp left jabs and watching out of the corner of my eye as this coach looked on disapprovingly. No way was I going to change my style now. I went back every day for the next week, and thought to myself how I actually missed being away from boxing.

After going to the gym for a couple of weeks, I finally had the confrontation with the Fort Waynewright coach. Once again he tried to change my jab as I pounded the heavybag. "Your jabs are taking too long to find the target," he criticized. "Shorten them up."

"Hey," I countered, "My boxing style was good enough to win the Chicago Golden Gloves tournament last year and I don't plan on altering it for anyone." That didn't go over too well.

"It's my way or the highway," said the guy. "Take Bubba over there, he's the best heavyweight in Alaska and if you use that slow jab of yours against a fighter like him, you'll get torn apart." I thought to myself, Alaska is known for exporting many great resources, but none of those were heavyweight boxers. I looked Bubba over and said I'd be happy to put on the gloves with him anytime. Suddenly the gym had become eerily quiet. Bubba was the king here, and he felt threatened by my offer.

He came over and got right in my face. “Punks like you wander in here from time to time with a big chip on their shoulder until I show them who is boss,” he said. “Now get your ass in the ring.” I laced up my gloves and then looked for a headgear. One of the locals said that against Bubba, one wasn’t going to do me any good. It was obvious everyone thought I was lying about winning the Golden Gloves.

The ring was in the back of the gym and everyone gathered around it for the impromptu grudge match disguised as a sparring session. I could tell by the look in Bubba’s eyes that he meant business. He had all of the support in the place, and everyone shouted words of encouragement to him. The bell rang. I came out circling to my right. Bubba tore right after me, firing wild haymakers with knockout intentions. I side-stepped his initial charge and popped him in the face with sharp, hard left jabs just like Nate had taught me. Bubba came charging in again, winging bombs at my head. I caught one on my shoulder and when I got in close I countered with a solid left hook to his chin and dropped him like a sack of potatoes. Once again silence reigned in the gym as the coach jumped in the ring and coddled Bubba. Both of their heavyweight championship dreams had just been shattered by one of my trademark left hooks.

That hook changed my life, too. That night I called Mr. O’Connor in Chicago and said I wanted to know more about professional boxing. “Craig, I think you’ve got the right style to make some money,” he said. “I also can find you the right manager.”

“Lets do it!” I said.

SIX

The trip to Alaska was nice, but it was great to be back in the Windy City. The first thing I did when I got home was contact one of my best friends, Jeff "Hillbilly" Davis, and off we went to Phil Smidt & Sons restaurant in Hammond, Indiana. The restaurant was known for the best-tasting frog legs in the world. If I was going to the electric chair tomorrow, frog legs from Phil Smidt & Sons would be my final request. Hillbilly filled me in on all that I missed the last few months. We had been tight since high school. He has mellowed greatly through the years, but believe me, in our early days we kicked plenty of ass together. Now Jeff has his act together and is one of the hardest workers I know. I am fortunate to say that Hillbilly is a true lifelong friend.

After our mouth-watering meal, I was relaxing at home when Mr. O'Connor called. "Craig, I'm thrilled to have you back. We need to get together and discuss our strategy for your professional boxing career," he said.

"I've got Jerry Lenza lined up to be your manager. He is currently working with local undefeated middleweight prospect, "Irish" John Collins, and has guided him near a top-ten ranking. I haven't told Nate about your plans, I thought I'd let you fill him in on all the good news. We have to get you together with Jerry as soon as possible."

Mr. O'Connor had become like a second father to me, and I knew that I could put full trust in him and any decision he made. Mr. O'Connor had that famed Irish gift of gab. He seemed to know everyone and had lots of connections. The stories he told of wining and dining international clients at Chicago's finest restaurants used to amuse me for hours. He was so different from my old man. Mr. O'Connor was always impeccably dressed, never a hair out of place, whereas my old man sometimes wore only suspenders without a shirt. With all of his tattoos you would have sworn he had on a paisley shirt under the suspenders. But, Mr. O'Connor and my old man really hit it off. They were both great guys from totally different backgrounds, but both were real and genuine.

I caught up with Nate at the gym. He was happy and surprised to see me. After the initial shock of my re-appearance wore off, we discussed my future as a professional boxer. "Nate, I'm ready to get started whenever you are. Mr. O'Connor has a financial backer all lined up for us," I told him.

"Craig, you are going to benefit from my past boxing experiences," Nate said. "I had almost a hundred professional bouts and when I retired I had little to show for it. I was always fighting for the short money. I had to box all the fighters that no one else would, just to earn a payday. In my first twenty fights, I fought guys like Tony Zale, Ken Overlin, and Teddy Yarosz, who held, or would hold, the world middleweight title. We're not going to feed you to the wolves. We'll take it one fight at a time. You are lucky to have a financial backer. I never had such a luxury. Craig, you have the guts and the work ethic to go far in this profession."

After a few wild nights on the town and catching up with family and friends, it was time to get down to business. Mr. O'Connor arranged a time to meet with Jerry Lenza.

> **Jerry Lenza (manager of Craig Bodzianowski):** *"Bill O'Connor was the person responsible for putting the deal together. I had known Mr. O'Connor for years. He had been a referee and a prominent man in Chicago boxing for quite some time. Because of the years of experience, Bill had a great boxing mind and he could be trusted as an individual. My first venture into boxing was being a member of a team of investors backing local undefeated middleweight prospect, "Irish" John Collins. At the time I was in the restaurant business and many of my customers followed John. Collins had a great fan base and I would sell up to 1,000 tickets for each of his fights right out of the restaurant. Craig Bodzianowski had built quite a local following from his success in the amateur ranks and Mr. O'Connor felt by adding Craig's current fan base, along with my boxing connections and fan support at the restaurant, we could make Craig a marketable and profitable boxer."*

The initial meeting went well. We never signed a formal contract, but had just a handshake agreement.

Legally, I could have walked away from Jerry at anytime, but the thought never crossed my mind. He always kept my best interest at heart. Our initial agreement called for a weekly salary and payment of rent. In return, Jerry would take a percentage of my fight purses after they reached a certain level. Jerry also got me a job working at his restaurant, Artie G's. I bartended, parked cars, and did anything else that needed to be done. Artie G's featured Italian food as its specialty, and I made sure our agreement included all the pasta I could eat. I had decided to start my professional boxing career as a heavyweight, and you can bet that I was seen at Artie G's loading up on carbohydrates quite frequently.

Everywhere I went, people wished me well in my new career. No one was more enthused than Nate. He sat me down and explained some of the differences between professional and amateur boxing. "You've got everything you need now to make it in this game," Nate said in that slow, soft voice of his. "Your rough, aggressive style is more suited for professional boxing than the amateurs. The rounds are longer and your fights will be longer than just three-rounds. You'll have to pace yourself more now, but the gloves are smaller so your punching power will be an even greater asset."

Nate was definitely my man. A lot of boxers switch trainers when they enter the pros, but I wanted to stay with Nate. He had brought me this far, and I was confident he could bring me to the top. He had coached hundreds of amateurs and some had gone on to professional careers, but Nate had never coached a contender. I planned on providing him that experience.

I went into serious training. I got up early for roadwork that consisted of a vigorous three mile run at maximum speed to increase my cardiovascular capacity. In the evening I would go to the gym and push my body to the limit six days a week, then rest on Sunday. I rotated workouts between the Woodlawn Gym near Nate's house and the Fuller Park Gym on Chicago's south side. Both were loaded with talented professional boxers who could provide excellent sparring to sharpen my skills.

Chicago was blessed with an abundance of talented heavyweights and cruiserweights in the Fall of 1982. I sparred with Alfonzo Ratliff. He had improved tremendously since we last swapped leather; so had I. Another sparring partner was undefeated Floyd "Jumbo" Cummings. This was one intimidating S.O.B. Cummings was an unbelievable physical specimen, weighing close to 235 pounds and standing 6' 2", with only a 32-inch waist. He appeared to be chiseled from granite. The year before, "Jumbo" had fought "Smokin" Joe Frazier right here in Chicago. Cummings knocked Frazier all over the ring, but only got a draw for his efforts. It was the legendary Frazier name that salvaged a draw for the former world heavyweight champion. After their meeting, Frazier retired for good. "Jumbo" and I had some classic sparring sessions. Holding my own with a seasoned professional only increased my confidence level.

I also worked with heavyweight contender James "Quick" Tillis. Tillis had lost a decision to champion Mike Weaver in a shot at the WBA heavyweight title the year before. He was more of a runner and a slapper, but he presented a different style to spar against. Another sparring partner worth mentioning was "Young" Joe Louis who had lost in a bid for the world cruiserweight title. Nate always said that the harder you train in the gym, the easier the actual fight will be. I lived by this rule as I trained with Chicago's finest ranked fighters daily.

Jerry Lenza finally delivered the news I had been anxiously awaiting. "Craig, on October 16th you will be facing Lawrence Lo Presto," he said. "He is a rugged fighter with limited professional experience. Mr. O'Connor and I feel that he is the perfect opponent for your debut. He will be a stern test and will come to fight." It sounded fine to me. Jerry and Mr. O'Connor wanted my competition to improve with each fight. Feeding me a bunch of stiffs, or "tomato cans" as they call it in the fight game, might serve to inflate my record early in my career, but it wouldn't help me in the long run. They planned on throwing a variety of fighting styles at me to prepare me for any type of prizefighter.

My first professional fight was at the Bismarck Hotel in downtown Chicago. I had butterflies all day long. From my amateur days I knew as soon as the first bell sounded all of my anxiety would be gone. As I climbed through the ropes, I could feel the adrenaline flowing. I paced around, keeping my eyes focused on Lo Presto the whole time. I was confident as I stood in my corner waiting for the bell.

As soon as it sounded, I charged at Lo Presto. Lo Presto stood his ground and fired back. We waged war at close quarters until I fired a straight right hand followed by my patented left hook. Lo Presto fell backwards between the ropes and eventually landed outside the ring. The only part of him I could see was the bottoms of his feet. The referee gave him an extended count because he landed outside of the ring, but when he finally got up, Lo Presto indicated that he'd had enough.

I was happy about the first-round knockout and planned to celebrate with the 250 best friends of mine who'd bought tickets. I showered, changed, and prepared for a night on the town. I made sure to say good-bye to Nate, Mr. O'Connor and Jerry. Jerry congratulated me, wished me a good night out and advised me to stay out of trouble. I joked, "you actually think I might go out and get into a fight or something?" All three of them nodded their heads. "OK, OK, don't worry guys," I laughed. "I promise - no trouble. I'll behave." It was a promise that became increasingly difficult to keep as my reputation grew from Golden Gloves champion to professional prospect. It seemed like more and more idiots wanted to challenge me outside the ring. I had more than one encounter with some drunk with beer muscles. I soon realized the importance of keeping a low profile. I did my best to keep my street fighting days behind me. I had nightmares of getting sued by some fool who had started trouble with me. From past experience I also knew that a well-placed punch with a bare fist can cause a serious hand injury. From now on, I'd try to keep all my knockouts in the ring.

My second career bout was scheduled for December 18, 1982, against unbeaten David Townsend. On paper it looked like a total mismatch. Townsend was 10-0, weighed nearly 240 pounds, and had a six-inch height advantage. I heard a lot of whispers that I was in way over my head in only my second professional bout. Mr. O'Connor had arranged for Townsend as my opponent. He had seen Townsend fight before, and figured that with his size and soft midsection, he would be tailor-made for my aggressive fighting style. That was all I needed to hear. If Mr. O'Connor said I could defeat Townsend, it must be true.

The weigh-ins were scheduled at the Bismarck Hotel for 11 a.m. the day of the fight. I noticed Townsend instantaneously. He was hard to miss, being the biggest guy in the place. I advised him that I was looking forward to meeting him in the ring that evening.

A funny thing happened in between the weigh-in and the fight that night. I arrived back at the hotel around five p.m. to get prepared and was greeted by Mr. O'Connor and Jerry. "Craig, your fight tonight has been canceled," said Jerry. "Townsend claims he was involved in a car accident after the weigh-in, and that he suffered a concussion. We're going to try to reschedule the fight as soon as possible." I was furious. I had personally sold over 300 tickets for this fight. I thought about how hard I trained, giving up women, beer, and pizza for the past few months. I vowed that if I actually ever got Townsend in the ring that I would make him pay for every bit of it.

I spent the rest of the night hanging out and watching tough, undefeated brawler, Lenny LaPaglia, and my stablemate, John Collins, both score impressive knockouts to hype their cross-town civil war which would be taking place in the near future. I also had the honor of meeting former lightweight champ, Ray "Boom Boom" Mancini, who was the television commentator. But it was mostly Dave Townsend's face that stayed in my mind that night. I wanted him bad.

Our match was rescheduled for January 24, 1983, at the DiVinci Manor, an old, dusty, renovated dance hall on Chicago's West Side. Gang graffiti covered the walls outside this rundown building in one of Chicago's depressed neighborhoods. It was a big night for boxing in Chicago. The bouts were broadcast live via cable television on *Sports Vision*. The main event featured Lenny LaPaglia in his final tune-up before squaring off against my friend, John Collins.

In the dressing room, Nate wrapped my hands and I loosened up. Mr. O'Connor stopped by to wish me luck and give some quick advice. "Start working over

Townsend's body right from the opening bell. He won't be able to handle your potent body punches."

On my way to the ring I could hear voices chanting, "Gator! Gator!" I felt lucky. I had an incredible fan base for a one-fight preliminary kid. Entering the ring, I saw Townsend and greeted him. He towered over me, and it occurred to me that if this guy ever had to haul ass it would take him at least two trips. I had to look up to go eyeball-to-eyeball with him.

At the bell I came out aggressively, stalking Townsend, slipping his left jabs and countering with lead rights to the mid-section followed by powerful left hooks to his jiggly belly. I could hear the air coming out of him as I worked downstairs. Near the end of the round I shifted my attack to Townsend's head. I landed a booming right hand that landed flush on his jaw, sending him staggering down to the canvas on his big ass. I give the guy credit. Townsend beat the referee's count, and then the bell rang to end the round. I returned to my corner smelling victory. Nate splashed water on my face and told me, "He's all yours, son; he's hurt. Now go out and finish him."

I raced off my stool at the bell and continued my offensive attack. I pinned Townsend against the ropes and let go a two-fisted barrage of punches. Once again he slumped to the canvas. I knew he was ready to go. The referee knew he was already gone. Before Townsend could rise, the referee halted the bout.

I spent the rest of the night greeting my well-wishers and settling in a ringside seat to watch LaPaglia in the main event. In typical Lenny fashion, he made quick work of his opponent to seal the match against my pal, Collins. It was a fight the Chicago boxing community was anxious to see.

A few days after the Townsend victory, Jerry phoned with exciting news. "Craig, you're scheduled to fight Robert Obey March 7th, and it will again be televised by *Sports Vision*. They were very impressed with your last fight. The Collins - LaPaglia fight is also a done deal, and you're scheduled to appear on that undercard." I couldn't have been more thrilled, and went right back into serious training.

I usually weighed near 200 pounds for my early professional bouts. I was considered a small heavyweight, and the weight class underneath heavyweight—the new cruiserweight division—had a maximum limit of 190 pounds. I was confident that I could get down to the cruiserweight limit, but the job wasn't easy with Jerry Lenza as my manager.

Jerry's wonderful wife, Bennie, happened to be a phenomenal cook. Every time I stopped by their house, she always seemed to have something cooking on the stove. Jerry was always trying to pass off some spaghetti or an Italian sausage to me. It was his nature; Jerry was always a very giving guy. I knew if I was ever going to drop down a weight class, I had better stay clear of the Lenza household.

The match against Robert Obey was held at the American Congress Hotel in Chicago. Once again, I conceded a weight advantage to my opponent. But Obey only outweighed me by about five pounds for my first scheduled six-round bout. Obey was listed out of Columbus, Ohio, and had an unbeaten record in four fights and a nickname even odder than "Gator"—"Dropped the Bomb On Me." Al Berstein did the broadcast for *Sports Vision*. Soon after this, Berstein landed a job as boxing analyst for ESPN. We were both going up in the world.

Obey had decent boxing skills and appeared to be in top physical shape. He was a big, well-muscled heavyweight, but I planned to use my bruising body attack to wear him down. Obey came out shooting rapid left jabs that I slipped with crafty head movement and countered with shots to his mid-section. It was close for the first two rounds, but then my body punches started to tell on Obey, forcing him off his toes and making him a stationary target. In the third round, we stood toe-to-toe and traded power punches. Near the end of the round I connected with a left hook that sent his mouthpiece flying. Obey was tired and resorted to punching below the belt. Fortunately, I had on a large groin protector that absorbed most of his blows. As Obey continued to land south of the border, I became enraged, yet at the same time feared for my unborn children. Finally, at the end of the round the referee deducted a point from Obey. That wasn't enough punishment as far as I was concerned. In the fifth round I pummeled Obey on the ropes and caught him with a pulverizing left uppercut followed by a hard left hook. I kept throwing punches until the referee jumped in and stopped the fight. I kept a diary of my early fights, and later that night I proudly scribbled in my journal that I had "dropped the bomb" on Obey!

My early professional bouts were promoted by former World Boxing Association heavyweight champion, Ernie Terrell. He had lost his title to Muhammad Ali on February 6, 1967. My old man told me that Terrell was one of the few guys that ever managed to get under Ali's skin. Before their bout, Ernie always referred to Ali by his birth name of Cassius Clay. This infuriated Ali, and Terrell continued to call him Cassius Clay as much as possible before their bout. Maybe it was the wrong strategy. During the fight, Ali would throw his lightning combinations at Terrell and shout, "What's my name? What's my name?" Ernie managed to go the full 15 rounds. After he retired, he started promoting cards around Chicago. He did a hell of a job, but bigger things were brewing.

> **Jerry Lenza:** *"Our management team was doing the best we could to get John Collins national exposure. Collins defeated tough fringe contender "Irish" Teddy Mann by a hard fought ten-round decision. Mann's promoter, Cedric Kushner, was pleased with Collins's effort and contacted us about signing Collins to a promotional agreement. We realized Cedric Kushner's worldwide connections and felt it was the best strategy to further Collins's career. I also negotiated for Kushner to get Craig Bodzianowski fights on all of John Collins's undercards. Cedric Kushner put together the John Collins - Lenny Paglia extravaganza with Craig booked on the undercard."*

Cedric Kushner was beginning to make some big waves in the boxing world. I had a lot of respect for him. He came from nothing and made himself a top promoter. He was a sixth grade dropout from South Africa who came to the United States in 1971 with only $400 to his name, and worked any job to make ends meet. He cleaned swimming pools and even operated a Ferris wheel in New Jersey. Kushner broke into the promotion business by putting together a Steppenwolf concert in 1974 and then got into boxing. He eventually hooked up with fellow South African and heavyweight title contender, Gerrie Coetzee, and became a major international promoter. Getting involved with Kushner made my future appear even brighter.

My fight against Richard Scott on the Collins-La Paglia undercard took place less than two weeks after I stopped Obey. An incident in training almost cost me the opportunity to fight on this major boxing event. I was sparring with James "Quick" Tillis and the session became a little heated by the fourth round. I began to land heavy shots to Tillis's body. He winced as I dug a particularly hard left hook to his body, and tried to counter with a left hook. He missed with the punch, but he followed through with an elbow that smashed into my nose. My nose was broken and swelled to great proportions. I also had two black eyes. Mr. O'Connor suggested that I bow out of the Scott fight. He felt that I should only enter the ring nothing less than one hundred percent fit for action. I understood his concern, but reasoned that all fighters go into battle from time to time with nagging injuries. Besides, I didn't want to jeopardize the exposure that fighting on the Collins - La Paglia card would generate. The date for the bout was March 20th, and I vowed to be there, black eyes, big schnozz and all.

The biggest fight card to hit Chicago in years took place at the UIC Pavillion on Chicago's West Side. NBC - TV's *Sports World* was broadcasting it live. There were two main events. Along with the wildly anticipated Collins - LaPaglia match, former world lightweight champion Sean O'Grady, who was on the comeback trail, was fighting John "The Heat" Verderosa. O'Grady was one of the classiest men to ever lace up the gloves. Years later, Sean became a boxing analyst for the USA Network and called several of my fights live on national television. He had forgotten that we had fought on the same card once.

Sean O'Grady (former world lightweight champion and USA network boxing commentator): *"I was only in Chicago a few days for my bout with John "The Heat" Verderosa. I didn't pay attention to the undercard fights because my focus centered on my bout. At that time, Craig only had a few professional bouts and I was not aware of him. Years later, I became friendly with him, calling a few of his bouts live on television and spending a day with him conducting pre-fight interviews for the USA Network. He is truly one of boxing's most interesting and unique stories."*

My match with Scott was one of the first preliminary bouts that day. Nearly 10,000 fans packed the Pavilion. When I entered the ring, I could feel the electricity in the hall. I looked Scott over as we waited for the introductions. At first glance, he seemed to bear a close resemblance to legendary former world heavyweight champion, Joe Louis. I only hoped that Scott didn't possess Louis's punch! My plan was usually to go to the body to wear down my opponent, but I noted Scott's well-defined stomach muscles and thought body shots wouldn't hurt him. As always, Nate's instructions were to work the body, but this time I figured I knew better.

I snapped a succession of sharp jabs to Scott's face at the bell, and strictly head hunted for the entire first round. Between rounds Nate scolded me. "Where are your body punches? Throw body punches!" he instructed.

"Look at his stomach," I argued, "Body punches will not effect him."

"Craig, body punches!" reiterated Nate as the bell rang again.

I charged out firing shots to the head and body. When I buried a left hook in Scott's muscled mid-section, he grimaced in pain and I chalked another one up for Nate. I followed up my attack until the bell. I had Scott right where I wanted him and finished him off in the third round. The crowd was the loudest I had ever fought in front of. They were revved up for the Collins - La Paglia match. Now that I had finished my night's work, I was as excited as everybody else was about it.

The theme from *Rocky*, "Gonna Fly Now," blared in the background as La Paglia made his way into the ring. He was a devastating puncher who had won all of his nineteen fights all by knockout--14 of them in the first round! La Paglia was often compared to 1940's middleweight champ, Rocky Graziano, because of their whirlwind fighting style, Italian ancestry, and troubled past. Lenny had learned his trade on the streets, whereas Collins, who was also undefeated (26-0), had grown up in a much more stable environment. Collins was a classic stand-up boxer with power in both hands.

John had the best ring entrance that I ever saw. He had a huge entourage consisting of twenty guys playing Irish music on bagpipes, a large flag of Ireland, and leading the procession was a midget dressed as a leprechaun. The UIC Pavilion nearly exploded when Collins entered the ring.

Collins - La Paglia was a 10-round war. Collins consistently pasted his rival with crisp, accurate left jabs and followed with crunching right hands that batted La Paglia. John managed to avoid La Paglia's devastating punching power, and even floored Lenny in the closing seconds of the final round to cement the victory. It was a unanimous decision for John.

The card was a huge success for the city of Chicago. The only downside, from a personal standpoint, was Sean

O'Grady's KO defeat by Verderosa. It was the last fight of the former champion's colorful and distinguished career.

As for me, it was time for a vacation. I had been in the gym continuously for almost a year since returning from Alaska. Jerry phoned a few days later, still euphoric from my victory and that of John Collins. Jerry may have been the happiest guy in Chicago. "Craig, great fight," he said. "Your next bout will be in about two months, so take some time off, have a good time, and get some rest." It sounded good to me. I made plans for some small game hunting along with catching up on my social life.

I had recently moved into a three-bedroom bachelor pad with Hillbilly and Mike O'Connor, one of Mr. O'Connor's sons. One night we planned a small get-together that turned into a major bash. The house was packed with people. Cars were lined up on both sides of the street for blocks. The music was loud and the beer was cold. The party continued in grand fashion until there was a knock on the door. It turned out to be worse than a cop responding to somebody's complaint about noise. It was Jerry Lenza! Not exactly the person I wanted to see at that moment. I had a feeling this was not what he meant when he told me to take time off and have a good time.

> **Jerry Lenza:** *"I had heard that there was a large party going on at Craig's place, so I drove by to have a look. You could hear loud, blaring music from the street and the road was filled with cars. I was angry and wanted a word with Craig. When Craig came to the door, he noticed my disappointment. I was not against him having a good time. I told him that if someone he did not know at the party got caught with marijuana, or if the place got busted and underage drinkers were*

found, he would be blamed and the press would be sure to mention it in the papers. I felt that it was important for Craig to conduct himself in a professional manner. There was money invested in his bright future and I did not want it jeopardized. From that day on, I never had a problem with him again. He realized he was a gifted athlete and remained focused on the goal at hand."

It was tough at times staying in on weekend nights, knowing that my buddies were out on the town chasing women and having a blast. But I was advancing as a professional fighter and I realized the price I had to pay to make it in this demanding profession.

SEVEN

My brief vacation presented an opportunity to recharge my batteries. My next bout was scheduled for May 22nd, in Chicago, against Jessie Hicks. I knew nothing about him and planned to keep it that way. In training I prepared myself to be ready for any style, and when the opening bell rang I knew I would be ready for whatever game plan Hicks presented. The bout would be held at the Bismarck Hotel Pavilion and featured heavyweight, James "Quick" Tillis, in the main event and also my amateur rival, LeeRoy Murphy, who was nearing a shot at the cruiserweight title.

Tillis was a cowboy from Tulsa, Oklahoma who had relocated to Chicago to begin his professional boxing career. Tulsa had proved little opportunity for a potential heavyweight contender, so Tillis had to rely on former "Toughman" contestants and university medical students for sparring partners. His first day in the big city, Tillis stopped at the Sears Tower on a sightseeing tour. He set down his suitcase and looked up at the world's tallest building. When he reached down again for his belongings, they were gone. Welcome to Chicago, Quick Tillis!

Tillis had received a title shot in 1981, losing a decision to W.B.A. Heavyweight Champion, Mike Weaver, in Chicago. It was a fight Tillis could have won with more effort. He fought defensively and ran from Weaver for most of the bout. It amazed me that a guy would not fight his heart out to win the heavyweight crown. At the Bismarck Hotel, Tillis would attempt to get his career back on track for another shot.

Promoter Cedric Kushner made sure to book me on every fight card he promoted in the Chicago area. The night of my bout with Hicks, the place was packed. It seemed that everyone in the audience was dressed in red and white, my fight colors. Every time I popped my head out of the dressing room I recognized someone in the crowd. My mom and my sister, Donna, led the chants of "Gator!" that filled the auditorium. It was a special feeling knowing that, in only my fifth professional fight, I had the loyalty of most of the fans in the arena. Since I had sold a lot of tickets, the next step was to make sure my supporters got their money's worth.

Hicks provided a difficult test. He was a survivor with a granite jaw. Our fight went the entire six rounds, and I posted a unanimous decision victory. I pressured Hicks throughout, landing telling blows to his head and body; but he would not fall. I was content to keep my unbeaten record intact, but at the same time felt disappointed that my knockout streak ended at four. After the bout I mentioned my disappointment to Nate. He wasn't unhappy at all. "Son, the bouts that don't end in a quick knockout are the ones where you learn from as a fighter," he said. "Tonight you went six hard rounds with a man who would not quit. Now you know you can handle six grueling rounds. I'm confident that you will have many more knockout victories in the future." I left the Bismarck before Tillis's main event fight, feeling better about things. I noticed other people were leaving, too, which made me feel better yet. They had come only to see my fight. It was nice to be appreciated.

James Churn was my next opponent. He had not lost any of his thirteen fights, but I wasn't in the other corner for any of them. We met at the American Congress Hotel in Chicago and one of my former amateur rivals, James Finn, fought in the opening bout.

Finn had retired from boxing after losing to me in the '81 Chicago Golden Gloves finals, and headed straight for the nearest buffet. After a lengthy absence from the fight game, Finn decided to turn professional and even the score with me. He went so far as to form his own "Gator Hater Club." My own anti-fan club! Finn would show up at my bouts with homemade signs and campaign for a rematch. Mr. O'Connor reminded me that I was almost a main-event fighter, while Finn was merely a club fighter with one professional victory—an unimpressive win over a fighter named John Cox with a lowly record of 2-8. Fighting a novice like Finn would be a step in the wrong direction for me. He felt I would learn more by boxing respectable prospects on their way up, like James Churn. I was happy to fight Finn again, but the decision was out of my hands. I let my management team book my fights. I just got in shape and showed up to kick some ass.

The Churn fight was a big step in the right direction. He was a shrewd, highly skilled boxer, but my relentless style wore him down. My steady body attack took the steam out of Churn and forced him to give up in the fifth round.

In the main event, Angelo Dundee's fighter, Ian Clyde, lost a twelve-round decision. It wasn't often that a boxer trained by Dundee lost a fight. It was an honor to have the legendary trainer in the house. He had guided Muhammad Ali and Sugar Ray Leonard to storybook professional careers after they had each won Olympic gold medals. I could not help but think how fortunate Dundee had been to inherit such talented fighters. Nate Bolden never had an Olympic boxer knock on his door looking for a professional coach. He had spent most of his coaching career teaching inner-city kids how to defend themselves—encouraging them to stay off the streets. If anyone ever deserved a gold medalist to train, it was Nate.

I felt like getting out on the town to celebrate my victory over Churn. It seemed that the more I progressed as a boxer, the more trouble I got into when I went bar-hopping. There always seemed to be some drunk who wanted to try his luck against me. Fortunately, these encounters were broken up before any damaging punches could be landed. My hands were considered dangerous weapons, but like anyone else there are limits to my patience. My boundary of tolerance tends to be quite small when the bullshit is headed in my direction. Somehow word always got back to Jerry and Mr. O'Connor about any mishaps involving me out on the town.

> **Jerry Lenza:** *"Craig was climbing the ranks in the boxing world and once again I warned him that we couldn't afford the negative press his bar fighting would generate. Craig promised to do everything possible to avoid an altercation. Craig used to start plenty of trouble in his younger days, but he realized the importance of his career and had matured greatly in the last year."*

After the Churn fight, I headed to a few south-side taverns to celebrate. I was having a blast chugging down a few well-deserved cold beers and enjoying the company of friends and fight fans when all of a sudden the trouble I wanted to avoid found me. I ran into a guy I wrestled with in high school who I hadn't seen in years. He was with a large muscle-bound man. The steroid freak pointed at me and stated, "This is the boxer you're always talking about? He don't look that bad to me." Then he said to me, "You're nothing Bodzianowski. I could wipe you out anytime." I remembered the promise I had made to Jerry and Mr. O'Connor and did my best to control my short temper. I looked this redneck up and down, taking in his proportionately large beer belly, and knew this idiot wouldn't last a round in the ring. I bit my bottom lip and turned away. "Bodzianowski, you're a sissy," prodded the beer-gutted musclehead. That touched a nerve. I had been accused of being a lot of things in my life, and some of the accusations even had merit, but a sissy I was not. I spun around and planted a left hook right in the bread basket. There wasn't much muscle there. Slowly, the muscle-head slumped to one knee, and then I gave him a shove and he tumbled over on his backside—much to the amusement of everyone in the tavern. Not so amused, were Mr.O'Connor and Jerry Lenza when word of the incident reached them, as it invariably did. It was time for me to develop new interests out of the ring.

Bill Donne, one of Mr. O'Connor's best friends, convinced me to join him whenever I felt restless. Mr. O'Connor had told him of my latest trouble, and Bill wanted to help out. I always enjoyed being with him. Even though almost forty years separated us in age, we always hit it off. Bill would take me golfing or to the shooting range, and sometimes we would go on weekend hunting trips. Bill did his best to keep me out of trouble. He even told me that when we hung out, it made him feel young all over again.

My professional record now stood at 6-0, with five wins coming via knockout. I felt confident that I was only a few years away from championship fights and big purses in what many considered to be the most demanding and difficult profession of all. Former middleweight champion, Rocky Graziano, once said boxing was the only profession in which a guy is almost guaranteed to end up a bum. Not for this 'Gator'. I could always fall back on hard labor or work as a tattoo artist, a profession I was learning to master from my old man. But that was for another time. Now all my thoughts and efforts were aimed at advancing my boxing career. I continued to train hard every day. Nobody ever had to come looking for me at workout time. Except once.

Late one morning after a long run, I was relaxing at home. It was a beautiful hot summer day, and my next bout was several weeks away. Hillbilly entered the living room and suggested we head to a crowded Lake Michigan beach for some fun."Can't do it, Hillbilly," I said. "I've got to meet Nate at the gym at 2 o'clock."

"Come on, Gator," pleaded Hillbilly. "Imagine all the babes out on a day like today. There'll be string bikinis jumping around all over the place." After a brief debate, I conceded defeat and planned to join Hillbilly at the beach. It was the line about the string bikinis that sealed the victory. My fondness for the opposite sex was the only thing that rivaled my love of the sweet science.

"First I have to call Nate and give him some justification for missing training today," I told him.

"Nate, it's Gator. I have a bad stomach ache and won't be able to make practice today." It wasn't original but I was in a hurry.

"You probably have some extra gas in your system, son," Nate responded.

"Yeah, that must be it. I'll see you tomorrow," I said, trying to hurry him off the phone. But you didn't rush Nate.

"Wait a minute, son. Go to the store and get yourself some 7-UP and call me back in ten minutes," he said. I had been through this routine with him before. I knew that when I called him back he was going to have me chug down the 7-UP, so after agreeing to get the soda, I hung up the phone. I filled up a pitcher of water and grabbed the remote control, channel surfing as Hillbilly paced the room, dying to get to bikini land. After ten minutes, I called Nate back and said I had the 7-UP. As expected, he told me to start chugging right then as he counted to ten. I did—only it was water not soda. When he finished counting, Nate yelled "STOP!" at the top of his lungs and demanded that I belch as loud as possible to relieve myself of the fictional excess gas. We repeated the process several times, and each time his count reached ten I let out the loudest fake burp I could muster. After the sixth time I finally convinced Nate I felt better. I thanked him and hung up the phone. Hillbilly was ready to roll but as I rose to my feet, I could feel all the water I'd drunk sloshing around. I sank back down on the sofa. "Hillbilly, I feel so water-logged I can't even move," I groaned. "Sorry, but I'm not going anywhere." I rolled over and fell asleep. A few hours later I got up and took the longest whiz of my life and headed to the gym for a workout. That was the last time I tried to pull a fast one to get out of training.

In the summer of 1983, I purchased a Kawasaki 440 with my purse money. Talk about your fateful investments. My old man was livid and immediately got on my case about my purchase. Considering he had once owned a cycle, it was difficult to see his point of view. Jerry and Mr. O'Connor also rode my ass about getting rid of the bike. I had too much to risk if injured in an accident, they argued. But I was going to win this one. I was keeping the cycle—end of story.

I was glad to hear my next match was scheduled for eight rounds, because more rounds meant more money. The fight would again be featured on *Sports Vision*. The phone never stopped ringing with ticket requests. It was around this time that my teammate John Collins suffered his first professional loss. He was blasted out in two rounds by former world title challenger, Tony Sibson, the European middleweight champion. The loss derailed John's hopes at a shot for the title. His defeat made me work even harder to avoid the same fate.

My workouts got more intense. One sparring partner in particular, Alan "The Mule Man" Alexander, always provided me with a difficult and sometimes unique sparring experience. Nobody wanted to work with the "Mule Man". Alexander was only a super-middleweight but in the gym he was the roughest, dirtiest, fighter I ever came across. Even the heavyweights in the gym wanted nothing to do with him. Our sparring sessions always turned into all-out wars. I'll never forget one of the last times I sparred with him, when Alexander was up to all his old tricks. The bell rang to end the first round of our heated session. About five seconds later, as I walked back to my corner, "Mule Man" hit me from behind with several jarring left hooks. "You S.O.B., try that again and you're history!" I shouted at him.

Mule Man looked at me calmly and said, "Gator, in the pros you've got to be ready for anything." Alexander also routinely used elbows, head butts and kidney punches in the ring. That's why he had difficulty finding sparring partners. He was a tough, inner-city guy who fought his whole life just to survive, and then used the same street style in the ring.

In the second round I came out winging punches, fueled by anger. Every time I caught him with a solid shot, "Mule Man" just grunted and sneered. I think he actually enjoyed taking punishment. When the round ended, I held up my gloves high to protect myself from another late shot, and said. "Come on Mule Man, hit me now when I'm in front of you." He just smiled and headed for his corner. I turned and started for my own corner when all of a sudden, wham! It felt like a thousand camera flashes were going off right before my eyes. I stumbled forward and then whirled around to confront the bastard.

"You've got to be prepared for anything, Bodzianowski," said Mule Man again.

"What I am prepared to do," I answered, "is kick your ass right now." Nate and some other trainers tried to end it then, but realized it was hopeless. This had turned into a real street fight. "Everybody get your ass out of the ring. I am going to kill this S.O.B.," I yelled. We battered each other senseless with punches for over ten minutes. Then my high school wrestling skills kicked in and I got the "Mule Man" twisted up like a pretzel. That ended it. Later, Alexander actually came over and congratulated me on a great fight. To me it had been the real thing, but I shook his hand. What the hell..."Mule Man" went on to notch several pro victories, but an eye injury prematurely ended his career. I honestly believe that with a bit more experience, Alexander would have given middleweight champ, "Marvelous" Marvin Hagler himself, all he could handle in a fight.

My next ring appearance under the Marquis of Queensbury rules occurred a few weeks after the Churn fight in a preliminary bout on a card headlined by Lenny La Paglia. It was La Paglia's first bout since losing to John Collins.

My opponent, Leonard Brandon, might as well have been Leonard Bernstein. I blasted him out in the second round. The LaPaglia fight took everyone by surprise. Lenny's previous fight against Collins had been total war, with LaPaglia absorbing plenty of punishment, but fighting back until the final bell. But this time La Paglia appeared to flat-out quit. He literally walked away from his opponent, Danny Blake, claiming he had been struck by a few low blows. To make it worse, Lenny was winning the fight up until then.

It was totally out of character for a tough grunt like La Paglia. The crowd at Di Vinci Manor booed him loudly, and he needed a security escort on his way back to the dressing room.

Boxing was such an unpredictable sport. I was lucky to have my whole family involved in my career. My sister, Donna, was in charge of my fan base. She helped line up buses before each bout that safely carted my party-minded backers to and from a few local bars. Each tavern sponsored a busload of fans. My other sister, Denise, sat next to Mom through all of my battles. Mom was probably my craziest fan. She would paint her fingernails red or whatever other matching color my fighting wardrobe was for that particular evening. My brother, Howard, would escort me to the ring and help in my corner. Howard is a big S.O.B. and was a great guy to have around in case trouble broke out. Kenny was always in the front row yelling his ass off for me. For the sake of everyone's well being, we left the old man at home on fight nights. He hated large crowds. We realized that with his quick temper, he and everybody else would be better off with Dad passing on my fight results to all the relatives and friends who phoned him at home.

My weight continued to drop a few pounds with each fight. For my next bout I weighed just under 190 pounds. Verne Bridges was a tall, well-muscled journeyman boxer from Ohio. As I climbed through the ropes all I could hear was a loud "Gator!" chant. It seemed as if half of the south side was on hand. The other half was watching the fight at home on *Sports Vision*, the local cable sports channel on which I was becoming a regular.

Bridges came out moving and jabbing. I noticed that when he threw his jab, he would bring his left arm back low, leaving his face exposed. I started countering him with overhand rights that repeatedly found the mark. Bridges started to hold me each time I connected with an accurate shot. I could hear my fans yelling with each punch I threw. It was "Gatormania" at its finest.

Midway in the second round, one of Bridges's sharp jabs bloodied my nose. It was the first time I had bled in a professional contest. He would pay for that. I picked up my offensive attack and pursued Bridges with reckless abandon.

I kept applying more pressure, and in the third round I caught him against the ropes and fired away, determined to end the fight with each power shot. Blood was splashed all over my face and I just wanted to end it as soon as possible. I stung Bridges with left hooks to the head and body, and mixed in a few solid right hands. He was out on his feet when the referee jumped in to stop the fight. I was covered in my own blood and relieved the fight was over.

My team kept me on a busy schedule for the rest of the year. I returned to *Sports Vision* and knocked out John Words in one round. Words was willing to trade punches, which played right into my hand. A solid right hand sent Words' mouthpiece flying into the third row. Then a devastating left hook almost sent the rest of him after it. Al Bernstein interviewed me after the fight. He asked more questions about my Gator tattoo than my fight. Al's major concern seemed to be what I would do if my Izod alligator ever went out of style. "It's a chance you take, Al," I informed the soon-to-be famous fight analyst. Then I smiled and winked into the camera. I love show business.

Ron Draper had over thirty fights on his resume in a ten-year career. His first professional opponent was the one-time "Great White Hope", Duane Bobick. Draper had also battled Big John Tate and Tony Tubbs, both of whom went on to claim a portion of the heavyweight title. He didn't beat those guys, but the veteran journeyman provided me with the biggest scare of my young career.

The fight itself, held three weeks after the Word match, wasn't much. I landed a perfectly executed left hook followed by a right hand on top of Draper's head. He crashed to the canvas and the referee counted ten and raised my hand in victory. My left hand was raised because the right one felt broken. But that quickly became a secondary concern as my cornermen lifted me on their shoulders for a victory lap around the ring. I looked down and realized Draper hadn't moved at all. The ringside doctor was desperately working him over to help him regain consciousness. Draper was just lying there, shaking a bit. I always took pleasure in my ability to put guys to sleep, but ten seconds at a time was long enough. I was scared and said a silent prayer. Draper slowly regained consciousness and seemed to be fine. I knew boxing contained major health risks for the guys wearing gloves, but I never wanted to be responsible for taking another man's life.

My right hand throbbed in pain. I couldn't even shake hands with anyone. Necessity is the mother of invention, and right then I invented my infamous Gator handshake which consists of tapping knuckles using only my index finger and middle finger. My right hand still tends to swell easily, and this handshake is less painful for me than a conventional one.

> **Jerry Lenza:** *"Mr. O'Connor and I got together to discuss the next direction to take with Craig's career. Craig would do anything Mr. O'Connor suggested and we decided that he was ready for his first main event bout. We decided on world-class globetrotting fighter, James Dixon, for Craig's next opponent. Dixon had fought in England against light heavyweight champion, John Conteh, and has also faired well against such highly-skilled fighters as Tony Tucker and Eddie Mustafa Muhammad."*

I was excited to headline my first professional boxing card, but first I wanted to try my hand at acting. Lawrence Tero, better known as Mr. T., the bodyguard-turned-thespian, co-star of "Rocky III", was in town to shoot a film called "The Toughest Man in the World." Mr. O'Connor not only arranged for my acting debut but also negotiated a small part for himself in the deal. We each got paid $45 a day, the going rate for non-speaking parts. I appeared as a boxer, surprise, surprise, and can be seen in the film working out in the background as well as sparring in a few scenes. When the cameras were rolling I made sure to land crisp, picture-perfect punches against my sparring partner. I had originally hoped for a small speaking part to use as a possible launching pad for a small-time acting career. But, what the hell, it was a lot of fun and I can always say that I appeared in a movie. There were bigger things to think about right then anyway.

James Dixon was known for his durability and strong chin. I figured our fight would go into the later rounds and prepared accordingly. My preceeding matches had been early knockouts. This one we prepared as if it would be a 15-round championship bout. I sparred daily with "Mule Man" Alexander (being very careful at the end of the rounds!) and Alfonzo Ratliff. Ratliff was then the third-rated cruiserweight in the world. But I noticed how much I had improved, too, since we last swapped leather in my amateur days. I knew that Dixon had much more experience and knew all the tricks of the trade. My plan was to go in and just out-box him, not necessarily looking for the knockout, but of course taking it if the opportunity presented itself.

What had been anticipated as a great learning experience for me ended up being a frustrating one. Dixon held and grabbed, intent only on survival and not winning. A few well-placed left hooks by me took the fight out of him. It's hard to look impressive against a guy who won't fight back. Between rounds even Dixon's cornermen pleaded for him to start fighting back.

Early in the seventh round I scored with a hard left hook that took any steam Dixon had left right out of him. He held on for dear life. The last time somebody hugged me so much in one night was at my senior prom, and she was much better looking than Dixon. When the bell ended the seventh, Dixon's cornermen ended the dance. Although Dixon had not been a very game fighter, it was another win on my record, and I was officially a main-event fighter.

Promoter, Cedric Kushner, was pleased with my progress. Kushner was gaining momentum as a force in boxing. He now had a heavyweight champion under contract. Gerrie Coetzee had shocked everyone with his dramatic knockout over heavily favored Michael Dokes to win the W.B.A. heavyweight belt. Coetzee's career had skyrocketed since he had signed on with Kushner. After two unsuccessful attempts at the heavyweight crown, Coetzee finally got it right. Next up for him was a mega-fight title unification bout against long-time W.B.C. heavyweight champion, Larry Holmes.

The Holmes-Coetzee extravaganza was scheduled for June 8, 1984 at Caesar's Palace in Las Vegas. I was slated to fight again on April 14th, and Kushner told me Jackie McCoy, Coetzee's trainer, would be in town for it. If I looked impressive, the promoter said I would be sent to California as a sparring partner for Coetzee. That was a big incentive against Frank Draper, no relation to recent knockout victim Ron Draper, and I got another one when Draper opened his big mouth at our weigh-in.

I remember his exact words: "Honkey, I am going to knock you out." I was used to ethnic slurs. Most of my close friends often referred to me as a "Polack," and that never bothered me. It was the fact that Draper thought he could upset me with his mouth that, well, upset me. I planned to jump on the big mouth at the opening bell.

Mr. O'Connor told me to forget about it and to keep a level head. I got hold of myself and promised to use my head. That lasted until I climbed through the ropes and Draper got back in my face screaming obscenities. The referee had to break us up before the fight even started. As soon as the bell rang, I raced out thinking knockout all the way.

Less than two minutes later it was over. I stunned Draper with several body punches and crunching left hooks. He went down three times before the referee stopped the slaughter. At ringside, Jackie McCoy was smiling and giving me a thumbs-up sign.

> **Jerry Lenza:** *"Mr. O'Connor was exuberant about Craig's acting as a sparring partner for world heavyweight champion, Gerrie Coetzee. Mr. O'Connor felt that Craig was ready to make his move toward a top ten ranking and that the trip to California would only help him as a fighter."*

Just a few days before the California trip, I received a call from Mr. O'Connor. He sounded choked up, and with good reason. Nate had been seriously injured in an automobile accident and was in the hospital. I jumped on my motorcycle and headed out to meet Mr. O'Connor to see Nate at the hospital.

Nate looked horrible. His face was grotesquely swollen, but he wasn't in any danger. He explained that his little mutt had gotten out and was running around in the street dodging traffic. When a car came flying around the corner heading right for the dog, it froze in the middle of the street. Seeing this, Nate instinctively jumped right in front of the oncoming care to rescue his dog. The car slammed on its breaks and skidded into Nate, who went flying and landed on his head. Can you believe it? Nate took the bullet for his dog. He loved that mutt so much.

California was out for Nate. “Craig, work hard out there,” he told me. “I’m sorry I won’t be going with you. You know I’m not much for travel anyway. I’ll be in good health by the time you get back”

Mr. O’Connor and I got together again just before I left for the West Coast. He was so thrilled with this opportunity. “We will have you boxing for a world title within a year, Gator”, he said. I had no idea then that I would never see this fine man, my second father and best friend, again.

EIGHT

LeeRoy Murphy and his trainer, Tom Fornarelli, accompanied me on the flight to California. Murphy was under contract to Cedric Kushner, and would be sparring with Gerrie Coetzee as well.

We stayed in Long Beach, and trained daily at nearby Westminster Gym. Fornarelli knew my weaknesses and strengths. Coetzee needed sparring partners with strong left jabs because Larry Holmes had the best jab in the business. I planned to show mine to Coetzee plenty of times when the opportunity presented itself.

It was early spring and a hell of a lot hotter in California than it had been in Chicago. Tom, LeeRoy, and I shared a three-bedroom apartment. Everything was strictly business—no sightseeing, no Disneyland, no California blondes, just boxing. We played a lot of chess and checkers to kill time in the evening and between workouts. Tom thought the concentration required by these games would sharpen our minds, but it mostly thinned out his wallet. Nobody ever beat me at checkers!

Tom woke us at six a.m. for our daily morning run. There was a high school football stadium nearby with a quarter-mile running track. We would jog a few miles and then run the stairs in the stadium. I was sweating my ass off. After our run we would rest up for our afternoon workout at the gym. I lost close to fifteen pounds my first two weeks in California. I felt I was in the best shape of my life. Jerry Lenza had just arrived in California, and planned to be at the gym the next day to watch my first sparring session with champion Coetzee.

The next day I arrived at the gym early. It wasn't every day a guy had the opportunity to trade punches with the world heavyweight champion, and I wanted to be prepared. I wrapped my hands and started to loosen up. After a while I became impatient and started to work the heavy bag. Almost two hours elapsed, and still no Coetzee. LeeRoy and I finished our workout and headed for the showers. "I guess when you are heavyweight champ you only have to show up at your own convenience," LeeRoy remarked.

We dressed and were headed out when a large crowd, made up mostly of reporters and cameramen, arrived filling the gym. Coetzee had finally arrived, and now wanted to spar. His total disregard for both Murphy and me ticked me off. I was more than willing to give the arrogant S.O.B. a go.

Jerry Lenza: *"I told Tom Fornarelli that I didn't want Craig to spar with Coetzee that day. It was Coetzee's first day in camp and several* *reporters were on hand to witness his initial workout for his upcoming bout with Larry Holmes. Craig had just finished a grueling workout and I feared that Coetzee would take advantage of Craig and show off for the press in attendance. Tom argued that Craig still deserved the opportunity he had waited for. Craig demanded to spar, so I gave in to both of their wishes."*

Coetzee was taller and larger than I had expected. He weighed close to 225 pounds, but that didn't concern me. I climbed through the ropes, bumping into several reporters who filled the small gym. As soon as the bell rang, I circled to my right in an attempt to avoid Coetzee's powerful right hand, which had been broken nine times until surgeons had fused the bones. Now boxing writers called it Coetzee's "bionic right hand." I boxed patiently, not loading up on my punches. It was only a sparring session, but I sensed that Coetzee was beefing up his punches for the benefit of the media. I slipped a few of his power shots with tricky head movements, and defensively caught a few rolling off my left shoulder. The jerk was obviously going for a knockout, which pissed me off and forced me to step up my own offensive attack.

Jerry Lenza: *"Craig and Coetzee both started to trade heavy shots. This was only supposed to be a sparring session. Craig gave up too much weight and experience to be going all-out with Coetzee. My worst fears soon became a reality. Coetzee landed a solid right hand flush on Craig's jaw. His eyes got glossy and he slumped to one knee. Craig shot right back up and* *charged Coetzee. I grabbed Tom Fornarelli to get his attention and demanded he stop the sparring session. Tom argued that to stop it while a round was still in session would only anger and embarrass Craig. I agreed and Tom promised to stop it after the bell."*

It was only a flash knockdown, and was the first time I had ever been down in a fight, whether in the ring or on the street. I jumped right back up and resumed punching until the bell ended the round.

Jerry Lenza: *"As Craig headed over to us, I congratulated him on a good job and told him to hop out of the ring to give LeeRoy Murphy a few rounds with Coetzee. Craig looked me straight in the eye and said that he was not ready to come out, that he still owed Coetzee an ass whipping. For the next two rounds Craig stayed on the offensive and got the best of Coetzee. He had never looked better, and if you were scoring on points, Craig would have won the last two rounds. Both boxers traded their best shots. A few more of Coetzee's bionic right hands found Craig's chin, but Craig never flinched and always fired right back. Craig proudly jumped on to the ring apron and held the ropes open for LeeRoy Murphy to get in. Murphy looked at him and said, 'Gator, thanks for pissing off the champ. Now I have to spar him.' Craig just grinned."*

It was the only time I worked with Coetzee. The next day when I arrived at the gym, I was informed that Coetzee did not require my services anymore; he felt I was too small and he was afraid he might hurt me. What a thoughtful guy! I think what Coetzee actually meant was that he did not want to get his ass kicked by an unranked 180-pound boxer. He was, after all, the holder of the W.B.A. heavyweight championship.

I was disappointed, of course, but that night I completely forgot about Coetzee. Mr. O'Connor's daughter, Lee, called from Chicago. Lee and I had dated on and off and had gotten quite serious at once. She was sobbing uncontrollably. "What is it? What's wrong?" I asked.

"It's Daddy......... he's........ dead," she said. I couldn't believe it. It just did not seem possible. My best friend in the world was gone. It's something I still have a hard time talking about to this day. It was such a sudden death that I felt I would never recover from it. He was like a second father to me and the best friend anyone could ask for.

> **Jerry Lenza:** *"We got Craig on the next flight home. His training in California had been cut short a week and he planned to return to Chicago for all of Mr. O'Connor's funeral arrangements."*

Mr. O'Connor was laid to rest on April 24, 1984 at the Holy Sepulchre Cemetery near Orland Park, Illinois. I acted as a pallbearer and it was the only time anyone ever saw a tear in my eye.

My next fight was scheduled for May 9th, only two weeks after Mr. O'Connor's funeral. Some people suggested postponing it until a later date. But I knew that Mr. O'Connor would want me to fight, and that's what I planned to do. I also hoped that preparing for it would take my mind off his death.

Physically, I was in the best shape of my career; but my mind was a mess. I went to the gym every afternoon but couldn't get in the right frame of mind. I only went through the motions.

> **Jerry Lenza:** *"We should have postponed the fight. Craig, with good reason, could not get focused for his ten-round main event with tough journeyman boxer, Francis Sargent."*

I hoped the fight itself would temporarily get my mind off everything. It was a big night for Chicago boxing and for me. I shared co-feature status with my friend, "Irish" John Collins, who was continuing his comeback from his defeat by Tony Sibson.

I didn't know much about Francis Sargent before our bout, but I sure had a feel for him by the time it ended. He provided me with the toughest scrap to that point in my career. It was trench warfare throughout the entire ten rounds. Fortunately, my body attack took a toll on Sargent in the later rounds. I landed several thunderous left hooks that gave me a slight edge in the bout, but Sargent fired back with effective uppercuts and body punches that found their mark. Sargent pressed me hard until the tenth round, when I took over. I was awarded an airtight decision. My performance showed that I had not prepared myself properly for this fight. If I had been in the right frame of mind, I would have knocked Sargent out.

John Collins got himself back on track in the co-feature by knocking out James Winston in the first round. After the fights, I told Jerry Lenza that I was ready for a big money fight against a name opponent. I was undefeated in thirteen outings and felt it was time to start making my move to the top. Chicago had three highly rated cruiserweights in LeeRoy Murphy, Alfonzo Ratliff, and Young Joe Louis. I wanted to make it four. But it was time to hang out and get boxing off my mind for a while.

Jerry Lenza: *"A few weeks after the Sargent victory, I headed to Atlantic City to meet with top British promoter, Mickey Duff, who was booking fights for some of the large casinos. I was hoping to get Craig a fight with former light heavyweight champion, Mike Rossman. Rossman had recently won two close decisions in Chicago over Luke Capuano. Craig had sparred with Capuano several times and always more than held his own. I had asked Capuano his thoughts on a proposed Rossman-Bodzianowski fight, and he felt Craig had a great chance to win. I felt a victory over Rossman would position Craig for a title shot. We were hoping to get a CBS televised weekend fight. We felt that Rossman was on the downslide and that Craig would have handled him."*

Our house parties seemed to grow larger each time we had them. I remember meeting a gorgeous gal named Beth Anderson at one of them. I noticed her right away. What a knockout—and I knew a bit about knockouts! She was one foxy lady, and built like a ton of bricks. Beth soon became my steady girlfriend.

Jerry Lenza: *"Craig never had to chase women. They chased him. He had plenty of attractive females after him all the time. Fortunately, it never interfered with boxing."*

I occasionally took Beth out for a spin on my cycle, but when the old man heard about it, we got into it. He used to get so angry when I'd stop by on my cycle. "Someday you are going to get hurt on that damn thing!" he said. "You've got too much to lose." Finally, I had enough and gave in to his wishes.

"Fine, I'll put an ad in the paper and sell it," I barked back. Within a week I had the bike sold. My motorcycle had been sitting in the front yard with a large "For Sale" sign draped across it. I had just cleaned and polished it. Some kid fresh out of high school stopped by with an offer I couldn't refuse. He said it would take him a few days to gather the cash.

May 31st was a beautiful hot day with clear skies. Beth was on her way over. She always looked great in whatever she wore, and this time she had on a skimpy halter top and a pair of the shortest shorts I ever saw, leaving little for the imagination. I suggested one last cycle ride. The bike would soon be gone, and you couldn't ask for better riding weather or a better-looking companion. I figured we'd go check up on Bill Donne, who lived in nearby Olympia Fields. As much as I enjoyed Beth's revealing outfit, I knew old Bill would enjoy it even more. I had been dating her for a while and she had yet to meet Bill. Today was the perfect opportunity. I kicked away the "For Sale" sign, and we headed off for Olympia Fields.

Bill was waiting for us outside as we pulled in his driveway. After an hour of visiting, it was time to get back on the road for home. Beth hopped on my motorcycle and we started the journey back home. In just a few short moments, the accident those close to me feared might happen was going to become a reality. We cruised down Bill's driveway and headed down the street. About two blocks from Bill's house, I pulled behind a '76 Chevy. I followed along when the car slowed down and put on its signal to turn right and then picked up speed to pass the vehicle on the left side. All of a sudden, instead of turning right, the car made a left turn right into me.

I got to my knees and looked for Beth. She had been scratched up a bit but suffered no serious damage. When I tried to stand up, I fell down. It happened twice, so I looked down. No punch ever rocked me as hard as what I saw. My right foot was just hanging there. Blood was splattered everywhere and poured freely from the red mess which was once my ankle area. I was kneeling right near the other vehicle's driver window, and instinctively I punched my fist right through the glass, yelling at the top of my lungs, "Why did you do this, you idiot?" I was in shock and remember lying flat on my back looking at my foot again. It resembled a chewed Thanksgiving turkey leg. I knew I was in serious trouble. My foot had gotten caught in the car's back bumper and been nearly twisted off. I could hear the sirens in the distance as I lay helpless in the street.

A kind, elderly lady named Lillian Lapka came darting out of a nearby house. She calmed me down and applied a tourniquet to my leg, which was pouring blood. I never lost consciousness. The ambulance arrived in no time. Olympia Fields Osteopathic, the hospital where they took me, was only four blocks away. Bill Donne had heard the commotion and arrived at the scene. I remember sweating profusely, thinking about how this injury could affect my boxing career. I grabbed Bill by the arm and pleaded with him not to tell my old man what happened. My dad thought I'd given up the bike, and when he found out about the accident he would be beside himself with anger.

The pain started to hit while I was waiting to go into surgery. They had to call in a specialist, and I waited what seemed like hours. In the meantime they stuck a needle in my stomach and shot dye into my spleen to check for internal injuries. All those abdominal exercises helped in the ring, but not here. It took two people to push the needle through my stomach muscles!

I just sat in the waiting room worrying if my next fight would be postponed. Then my worst fears, of doctors not being able to properly fix the injury, crossed my mind. I had been taking some business courses at the local community college, but I was by no means ready to clip on a tie and jump into a business suit. I still had a lot more to prove in the boxing ring.

My mom was my first visitor at the hospital. The old man was still at work and had not yet been told about the accident.

Gloria Bodzianowski (mother): *"Mrs. Donne called to inform me of the accident. I got a ride to the hospital right away. Craig looked just awful. He had hunks of flesh missing from his arms and legs where skidding on the road just tore the skin right off. His right leg looked even worse; it was sheared right to the bone, no meat or nothing, just pure bone. However, at the time, amputation never crossed my mind. I called my husband from the hospital as soon as he arrived home from work. He was furious without really understanding the seriousness of the injury. He said he would get to the hospital as soon as he could. In the meantime, Craig was hauled off for what would be nine hours of surgery."*

Jerry Lenza: *"I was still in Atlantic City negotiating Craig's fight against Mike Rossman* *on national TV. I had a verbal handshake agreement with promoter, Mickey Duff, and with great excitement phoned home to my wife, Bennie, with the good news. She was uncharacteristically quiet. I knew she loved to play bingo as well as the slot machines, and figured she was still a little upset about not coming to Atlantic City with me. The next day I called again and got the truth about Craig's accident. I could feel my heart sink. I caught the next available plane home."*

I remember waking up from surgery and seeing my mom. I looked at my elevated right foot. There were metal rods sticking out of it and stitches everywhere. It was obvious that I would not be climbing into a boxing ring anytime soon.

Moments later, my old man came by. He looked at my leg and started crying. It was the first time in my life I had ever seen him cry. Then he started cussing. That I had heard before. He muttered words I'll never forget. "It's got to come off, damn it, the leg's got to come off." I laid my head down on the pillow and stared into space. I knew he was right. Dad had amputated legs on some of his fighting pit bulls, and when he said that about my leg, I realized it was doomed.

My hospital room felt like a morgue. I had a lot of visitors but was in no mood for company. I felt like I'd let everyone down. The daily paper ran an article that said my fighting days were over. I prayed for a miracle recovery, but my leg became infected and was turning black.

The doctors said I had two options. "Whatever one gets me back in the ring quickest is the one I'll take," I declared before they even told me what they were. "Craig, unfortunately your fighting days are over. We will be lucky to save your leg," one of the doctors said. Dr. Pelicore, who had done my initial surgery, said, "We can start what will be a number of surgeries over the next few days in an attempt to save your leg. At best, hope you will be able to walk with the use of a cane." That was the first option. "Or," he said, "We can go ahead and amputate." If they took my leg I'd never be able to fight again, I thought... until Dr. Pelicore mentioned that with a prosthesis I would be able to lead a life that included such activities as golfing and running.

I thought to myself that if I could run, then I could definitely box. I looked at everyone in the room, and then at Dr. Pelicore and said, "Adios, let's cut it off!"

NINE

I woke up after the amputation realizing life was going to be a hell of a lot different from then on. Immediately, I inspected the aftermath of the operation. I slowly picked up the covers and peeked underneath. As expected, half my leg was gone. As bad as it was, I knew I could handle it. Alongside the loss of my brother and the death of Mr. O'Connor, this seemed almost minor in comparison. The beliefs passed down to me in childhood would carry me through. As kids, when one of us got hurt and came home whining or crying, the old man would say, "What's wrong? It's not that bad! It's over, you're still alive; the worst part is behind you. Deal with it!" That's exactly the attitude I adopted now. I had to deal with it and move on with my life. The most difficult thing to do would be throwing in the towel, because then I would have to live with myself as a quitter, and that is something I never considered. Besides, if my fake leg was half as good as promised, I figured I might even get it to work better than the real one!

The removal of my right leg six inches below the knee necessitated filling my body with morphine and pain-killers. That really messed up my system. Right after surgery I vowed to leave the pain-killers alone. I had never done drugs of any kind and preferred to lie in my hospital bed and sweat gallons to taking morphine. I didn't want to risk becoming hooked on the stuff. My mom told me horror stories about people getting addicted to drugs after surgery. I was going to box again, and that was a chance I did not want to take.

> **Gloria Bodzianowski:** *"I thought to myself there is a God. This is not happening. I was the last face Craig saw before bed each night. He was in intensive care and on all sorts of medication. They made me sign papers for the amputation because he was on a heavy dosage of drugs. It was heartbreaking. As they wheeled Craig off to surgery, he tried to cheer everyone up by stating that he would be fine, and by promising to fight again."*

Family members, boxers, promoters, friends, girlfriends and ex-girlfriends visited me in the hospital. One of my biggest fears I had concerning the amputation was how it would affect my romantic life. Would I still be a hit with the ladies? I would not know until I got out of the hospital.

Jerry was one of my most frequent callers. I'll never forget his first visit. Jerry and Bennie stopped by with food in hand, including my favorite dish, linguini with shrimp. Jerry looked a lot more affected by the whole ordeal than me. He was sobbing and had a difficult time getting his words out.

Jerry Lenza: *"I had a difficult time seeing Craig for the first time after the accident. It appeared his boxing career was over, but I was more concerned with what was going to become of him. I was worried about him living with the injury. How was he going to react to this adverse situation? Here was an up-and-coming undefeated fighter, whom all of his peers looked up to with admiration. Now he was missing a leg. I feared for his confidence as a human being. I did not know if he could handle living with the loss of a leg, but obviously it was me who had a much more difficult time with it. I thought in my mind if they take his leg off, that will be the end of this kid. To see all his hard work go down the drain, I was afraid of what it was going to do emotionally to him."*

In an attempt to cheer Jerry up, I grabbed the bar suspended over my hospital bed and started doing chin-ups. "Hey Jerry, check it out," I said. "I can't get soft while I'm in here. Tomorrow some of my buddies are bringing in my hand grips and some free weights. I am fighting again. No doubt about it." I knew that Jerry, like everyone else, thought I was crazy. I felt that my brothers and sisters and a few close friends truly believed me, which was all I needed. It made no difference that there had never been a professional boxer with an artificial leg or that I heard rumors that there wasn't a chance in hell that any state athletic commission would ever sanction me to box again.

Jerry Lenza: *"At first I did not believe it would be possible for anyone to box with a prosthetic leg. I was not overly thrilled to hear Craig wanted to fight again. I feared he might actually be vulnerable in the ring. At the time I knew little about prosthetics. However, if Craig's heart was set on fighting, I planned to back him 100% because if I didn't, I knew he would find someone who would."*

The next day my pals, Chris LaBonca and Ray Sistino, dropped off my free weights and I started pumping iron immediately. I was in the best shape of my life before the accident, and I didn't want to go back too far. I felt bad for the guy sharing my hospital room. He was trapped in my mini-gymnasium. I knew it was only a matter of time before I drove him nuts.

It's true what they say about hospital food—yuck . Besides that, they did not give me enough. I usually got a few pieces of burnt toast, two overcooked eggs and a tiny fruit cup. The next time Jerry and Bennie came to visit I begged them to bring me some quality food from their restaurant. I could not stomach the hospital grub anymore. I gave my parents a list of items, including fruits and vegetables, to bring me on their next visit.

Under no circumstances would I allow myself to get down mentally. I thought back to some of the positive conversations I had had with Mr. O'Connor. One verse he always repeated stuck in my mind: "Whatever the mind can believe, the body can achieve." I felt they were words to live by. My foot was gone and there sure as hell was not any way another one was going to grow back. Shit happens. I could accept that; the problem was getting the doctors to accept my acceptance. Every day a psychologist dropped by to help me deal with my loss. My positive outlook was of great frustration to the resident head shrink. He informed me that a full recovery was possible only if I opened up and let out "my true feelings." He couldn't understand I was fine. My mind was made up about fighting again despite what others said, and I had nothing else to get off my chest. I complained to my mom about the unrequested visits from the shrink, so she advised me to tell him what he wanted to hear to get him off my back.

On his sixth daily visit, I decided to open up, at least in my own way. The conversation started the same way, with the psychologist asking how he could help me. "There is something you could do to really help me," I told him.

That got him all excited, and he asked, "What is it?"

"Could you help me hang a punching bag in here?" I said. "Nobody else will help me with this." The poor shrink just shook his head in frustration, and then left the room for good. I could not help laughing. I already knew my head was screwed on exactly right. Who needed him to confirm it?

Things were always a little uptight in the intensive care unit where I was stationed. I wasn't their usual patient. Fortunately for me, as requested, Jerry and Bennie brought plenty of great pasta to pass around to the hospital workers and all of my visitors. Jerry even slipped the security guard some mussels and linguini to make sure all my guests were given the best treatment.

Cedric Kushner telephoned while I was in the hospital. He sounded very nervous on the phone. "Cedric, I'm fine. Just plan to book me a fight soon on one of your promotions," I said. He went along with it, but I knew he thought I was loony. He told me it was not possible to box with one foot. I explained how it was impossible to fix my right foot, and if I wanted to fight again, cutting it off had been my only option. I knew I could not box using crutches or a cane. A fake leg was my only hope. I made sure that Jerry followed up with Kushner about my future plans. Kushner also told Jerry he was insane for even thinking such thoughts. I figured that Kushner should just step in line with the rest of my doubters. In my heart I was going to box again. Now I just needed to figure out how.

It was difficult to imagine life without boxing. On the inside, I knew I had plenty of fight left in me. I didn't think it was fair to be deprived of making a living the best way I knew how. I had some friends in business who had offered me jobs in the past. I never feared ending up washing dishes for a living. But, in the meantime, all my thoughts concentrated on returning to the ring.

The doctors promised I would regain up to 80% mobility in my right leg with the aid of a prosthesis, which was enough mobility for me. I was never considered too swift of foot before the accident—Fred Astaire I was not. A dancer like Sugar Ray Leonard might have a problem in the ring with an artificial leg, but I always moved straight ahead, only occasionally stepping to the right or left to cut off the ring on the other guy.

My weight dropped big time during my hospital stay, thanks to the food and my ambitious workout schedule. As soon as I was able, I walked long distances in the hospital on my crutches. I purchased a special, more comfortable pair of Canadian crutches that allowed me to scale three stairs at a time. On my final day at the hospital I weighed in at 157 pounds. I was mostly skin and bones with a little muscle thrown in. The loss of my leg accounted for a nearly seven pound loss, to go along with another fifteen that melted off during my stay. I could not wait to get the hell out of there. A few sports reporters interviewed me on my final day. I talked about my comeback plans, and jumped out of my wheelchair throwing punches at the cameras while hopping on my left foot. That night I arrived home just in time to catch my shadowboxing exhibition on the 10 o'clock news. It felt good to be back on TV!

After three weeks plus one day of confinement, I was happy to be a free man again. Moving back home with my parents wasn't my first choice, but it made sense for two reasons. I wasn't able to care for myself just yet, and I had no other place to go. During my hospital stay we had been evicted from our wild bachelor pad. The last party got so crowded that it had actually moved out onto the neighbor's roof. I heard it was a barn burner. Actually, the timing worked out well considering that I would be laid up for some time. At home my family circled around to help me, and my brother, Kenny, was good enough to give up his room to me. He slept on the floor.

A few things had changed since I last lived with my folks. My sister, Donna, had been through a difficult divorce and moved back home with her son, Jeffry. My nephew was only a few years old, but tagged along wherever I went. We became inseparable companions. Some things had not changed, chiefly the fact that the old man was still as temperamental as hell. The first time I heard his temper go off, I instinctively threw my arms up over my head in a defensive position. Old habits are hard to break!

My first evening back, I jumped on my crutches and headed out the door with Jeffry. I needed some fresh air. I waved to various neighbors as we proceeded along, and noticed everyone gawking at what was left of my right leg. They meant no insult; I'd have stared, too, in their place.

Our little jaunts became a daily ritual, as did what happened when Jeffry and I returned. Then, Jeffry would change my bandages and clean the stump of my leg. It was a thankless job, but that little guy would dig right in there and apply disinfectant directly to the wound. It was a job nobody else was willing to do. After he was finished, he would re-bandage the nub. Jeffry was a tremendous help.

> **Jeffry DeBauche:** *"I always wanted to be like my Uncle Craig. I did back then when I was a young kid, and I still do to this day. I remember when he moved back after the accident. Everywhere he went, I tagged along. One time I was lying out in the road, sticking my leg out at oncoming cars. My mom came running out of the house wondering what the hell I was up to. I told her that I was hoping a car would run over my leg so I could be like Uncle Craig."*

The phone never stopped ringing at my parent's house. Sometimes it was Beth or a buddy or a reporter, but other times it was some gal who had read about me in the paper. Heaven couldn't be much better. My first three weeks out of the hospital I was on a different date each night. Beth and I had cooled off during my hospital stay, which was okay. I kind of enjoyed playing the field. I would not recommend getting your leg amputated to improve your love life, but it was doing wonders for mine!

I joined a nearby gym called the Healthy Attitude Fitness Club, and continued to pump iron. There has always been the myth that boxers should not lift weights. Even Nate felt this way. But you can't tell me that guys like Ken Norton and Evander Holyfield—both heavyweight champs—never lifted a weight! It was a major concern of mine. I consulted gym manager and fitness expert, Ralph Suca, on the matter, and he helped me develop a regimen. We concentrated on a high volume of repetition which also enhanced my cardiovascular capacity. Ralph saw my dedication and helped me in every way. One of the craziest things I remember about those first workouts was the itching sensation I'd get in my right foot—the one that wasn't there anymore. I would even bend over to scratch it. These phantom sensations ceased after a few months. I ended up at the gym so much they offered me a part-time job selling memberships. I enjoyed sales and even qualified for a trip to the Bahamas. But my main focus was always attaining peak condition again.

Afternoons, I spent time with the Andrew High School swim team. I attended each summer practice as an honorary team member. My brother, Kenny, attended Andrew High, and knew the swim coach. When I was in high school, the coach had been the Sandburg High phys-ed teacher. Those summer practice sessions were a killer. I eventually worked my way up to swimming four miles a day. My conditioning program also included boxing workouts even though I still hadn't been fitted for a prosthesis.

Nate stood by me all the way. At first he did not realize I was getting a fake leg. Nate actually thought I would be boxing on one leg! The sad fact was that my coach was getting on in years, and senility was starting to set in. But when the subject was boxing, Nate was always on top of it. Nate guided me through a workout whenever I made it to the gym. On my return to the squared circle, Nate notified everyone that I would be hopping around the gym on one leg. As supportive as he was, I sensed the other boxers at the gym gave my comeback intentions little credibility. They wished me well, but I knew that they thought I was some poor bastard out of my mind. I couldn't blame them. I must have looked odd hopping around the gym on one leg, a boxer in training, intending to resume a career.

My hospital bills were substantial, and I wasn't covered by any health insurance plan. Fortunately, Cedric Kushner and the Chicago boxing community came to my support. Kushner staged a boxing card at the American Congress Hotel on July 25th in my honor, and each boxer on the card donated a large percentage of his fight purse to me. And, of every ticket sold, $50 went toward my medical expenses. The place was packed. There were a lot of people who came that night just to make a donation; adding to the sparse crowd that otherwise would have normally paid to see preliminary boxers at the local club shows. I needed the money to help fund my new prosthesis. This event also provided an indirect means for that.

I grabbed the microphone during a break in the action and addressed the crowd, "Thank you all for your support. This money will help a lot toward my expenses. I will be fitted for my new leg in a few weeks. I don't care what it looks like, I'm tired of walking around on my arms. I hope you can all make it back in a few months for my first fight." I was amazed how everyone came through for me. The publicity from the event resulted in a phone call from an orthopedist, Dr. Robert Eilers, who was willing to donate a prosthesis. Good things were starting to happen.

Bill Donne invited me to join him dove hunting with some friends. I told him that I would not get my new leg for a few weeks, but he wouldn't take that for an excuse. Finally, I gave in, praying that my aim was just as good on one leg. The hunt was a blast. I proved an even better shot on one foot. When I got on my knees, I rarely missed the target. In or out of the ring, this leg issue was not going to stop me. I figured it would only be a matter of time before I had two legs. The only difference between me and anyone else was that one of my legs happened to be store bought.

Finally, the day came to be fitted for my first prosthesis. Dr. Eilers prescribed one prosthesis that was designed and fitted by prosthetic specialist Mike Quigley of Oakbrook Orthopedic Services. I was straight with Quigley from the start. I appreciated his time and effort, but I said that if he wasn't prepared to get me the best leg possible, I would find someone who could. Quigley promised to get the best prosthesis available, and in return I would become his pet test project on improving the prosthesis for increased use. I was considered to be in the 99th percentile in both weight and degree of physical activity. This, therefore, made me an ideal case study. Quigley was outstanding. He never charged me a dime for parts or labor. In return, I visited many amputees at hospitals to lift their spirits and recommend them to Quigley.

Mary Hajduk: (assistant prosthetic specialist who worked with Mike Quigley)

"Clarence Imler was the first prosthetic specialist to work with Craig before Mike Quigley. Craig needed some revision work, such as having the end of his bone shaved down and his nerves tied before he could be casted for a prosthesis. Craig was a pioneer in the prosthetic industry. In 1984, when Craig became injured, he was one of the first people who dared to resume his life normally at a time when prosthetics were treated more like geriatrics. There had not yet

been much of a sports medicine approach to prosthetics. Since Craig first received his prosthesis, a lot has changed in the industry. In the late 1990's, there are now a lot of product sponsors who will financially back an amputee. This type of benefit did not exist at the time of his amputation."

Getting that leg under my ass for the first time was the best feeling in the world. My first device was the Flex Foot, a solid, single piece that was new on the market. It acted as an energy storage unit, the more I pushed it, the more energy it returned. Quigley warned me that my leg muscles would need to adjust to the new demands put on them, and I would need to take it very easy at first. He recommended walking on it for a half-hour the first evening and adding a little more time each day. It felt so good to get off those damn crutches! The new leg actually fit quite comfortably at first. I figured since I was still in top physical condition, the rules set for other amputees didn't apply to me. Quigley gave me a wear schedule to build up my prosthetic tolerance. Unfortunately, I ignored his advice and overworked my artificial leg in the beginning.

When I got back home, I paraded around the house showing off my new leg. I felt reborn. Kenny was home, and he said when I was up to it he wanted to challenge me to a racquetball game. Before the accident we played all the time and were pretty evenly matched. The past few months following my weight lifting sessions, I had picked up many pointers on racquetball by watching state champion, Jim Corcoran, play for hours at a time. "Let's go, right now!" I told him.

The leg and I were not yet quite in sync, but I moved surprisingly well. Even more surprising was that I held my own on the racquetball court, which wasn't bad for a guy who hadn't even walked in months. After playing for over an hour, I started to feel pain in the nub of my right leg and called it a night.

When I got to the locker room I took off my leg to inspect the damage. There was blood all over the place. The bone had broken through the skin and was sticking right out. Nice going Gator. I guess it was time to start listening to the specialists. Now I would be back to square one. I knew I had over exhilarated myself in this physical activity. It was a painful setback. The next day I returned to Mike Quigley's office to show him the damage.

When I saw him, Mike Quigley was not happy. I was told that this injury would require three months to heal. It was heartbreaking news, but I knew that I was the only one to blame. Instead of kicking myself in the ass (which would have been almost impossible anyway), I headed straight back to the gym for more weightlifting and cardiovascular workouts.

It was there that I met Mike Moe, who would become a close friend and very instrumental in my comeback. Moe knew nothing about boxing, but he knew a lot about fitness, especially weightlifting. We had the same workout schedule and we just really jelled with one another right away. He would push like there was no tomorrow.

After three months that seemed like three decades, it was time to give the prosthesis another shot. This time Quigley read me the riot act before fitting me with the leg. He was happy I had stayed in prime condition, and said I would require little physical therapy. But he emphasized that my calf muscles and skin would need to absorb forces about three times my body weight (which had risen to about 200 pounds) every time that I ran or jumped. I got the message, and there would be no racquetball game when I got home.

I did start jogging right away, and, naturally, I overdid it. My leg felt terrific the first few times I did roadwork, but the bone eventually broke through my skin again. I would have to wait out another three month sentence while the injury healed. Words can't explain—at least printed ones—the frustration I felt. Again I had to suffer through the waiting process. I returned to the gym minus a prosthesis and kept up my heavy fitness workload. I did not want any more setbacks, and the next time I saw Quigley, I not only listened harder than ever but even took notes. No way in hell was I going to wait any longer.

The third time was a charm. This time I gradually worked into condition, carefully following the guidelines prescribed by Quigley. I stuck to biking and swimming at first, and I only walked on the prosthesis the designated amount. Eventually I started jogging. It took some time to work my way up to a few miles. The only difficulty I had was when the elastic rubber sleeve on the prosthesis tore my skin off above the nub from too much friction. Then I would grease it up with Vaseline and continue running. It was a small price to pay to keep my conditioning routine on schedule.

Mary Hajduk: *"Craig was a real inspiration for many people. He was basically on a stilt on his right side and proved to many that life still goes on. Many amputees saw Craig as someone pursuing his dreams and they instantly were not as down on themselves. Craig would visit many amputees at the clinic and at the hospital to lift their spirit. Dave Renner was one such* *individual. Dave had lost his leg and part of his other foot in a train accident. Craig stopped by to see him several times in the hospital and inspired him to achieve success. Today, Dave is a prosthetic technician helping other amputees lead a normal existence."*

During my workouts at the Healthy Attitude, Mike Moe was pushing me to the limit. Moe was a dedicated power lifter and had me pumping heavy iron. I attribute an increase in my punching power from lifting with him. My strength had increased dramatically over the past few months. I remember one time dead lifting just over 500 pounds and actually bending my prosthesis under the weight. Thank God Quigley absorbed the cost of all my mistakes!

Mike Moe: *"I had never seen someone as dedicated as Gator. I was not a boxer, but we hit it real hard. Eventually, I started spending a lot of time in Gator's overall training process. At first I ran with Craig in the evenings, but I couldn't keep up with him. I would drive his jeep as he ran along side of it. I would not let him miss a day. He never even thought of it because if he did, I knew where to find him."*

My weight eventually reached 217 pounds and included a low percentage of body fat. I was one buffed S.O.B., which greatly disappointed Nate. With all my leg problems, I had been out of the boxing gym for quite a while. "Where did you get all those muscles?" he wondered as he got a look at me. My weight had ballooned too much from all the weight lifting. I had planned to resume my career at the 190-pound cruiserweight limit. To get back down there, Moe and I went on a 60-day tuna-and-potato-diet. The selected menu of choice got a bit monotonous, but it worked. I had actually ate my way back down to fighting weight.

But there were still problems getting my prosthesis to work well enough for boxing. It was a great invention, but the phony leg could not hold up under the constant punishment I dealt it. It was getting quite frustrating. I was snapping my prostheses left and right. One time I pushed off my right foot to throw a left jab and the damn thing broke. If that happened in a real fight I would be in more trouble than the proverbial one-legged man in an ass kicking contest. I needed a more durable leg. Fortunately, since I was Quigley's pet project, one was already in the works.

Using the latest space-age technology, Quigley, and Don and Shirley Poggi of Model + Instrument Development built me a unique spring-action prosthesis called the "Seattle Foot." The Poggi's had heard about me and offered their services. They flew to Chicago with their own engineer. I explained the problems I had with the first prosthesis and gave them specific information on what was needed to make this device a success.

The Seattle Foot was state-of-the-art. About 600 patients used it nationwide. One of them, Jeff Keith, ran across the United States on his Seattle Foot. The Poggi's wanted their customers to push their invention as far as possible to test its durability, and were constantly making adjustments and improvements. They modified several legs for me until I was satisfied.

The Seattle Foot provided a type of stored energy similar to the springy action of a diving board. The prosthesis wasn't stiff, and I could move it almost like a real limb. On top of that, it was authentic looking right down to the fake toes and realistic looking toenails. I could even wear sandals again.

There still remained the problem of finding an adequate and comfortable means of attaching the prosthesis to my nub. That was solved by a latex sleeve extended like a cuff tightly over the shin and above the upper edge of the total prosthesis, which provided a type of suction fit. A gel insert provided shock absorption. The Seattle Foot also offered a foot and ankle component that was extremely resistant to breakage—offering a foot that was strong as well as light in weight. I even added my own personal twist.

The Seattle Foot was bolted to a new invention described as the "Gator Leg," which naturally included a small Izod alligator. Made of durable fiberglass, the "Gator Leg" resembled a real leg.

Now with my prosthesis problem finally solved, I needed to get some ring work and prove to the Illinois Boxing Commission that even if I couldn't stand on my own two feet anymore, the ones I had would do just fine.

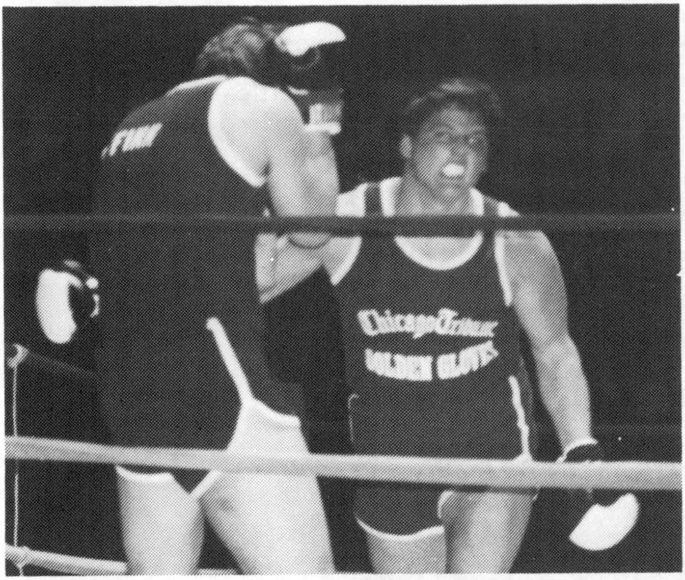

Craig "The Gator" Bodzianowski winning the Chicago Golden Gloves championship match against Jim Finn.

The Early Days
Craig's family.

Top:
Craig and Donna

Bottom row:
Denise, Howard,
Ken and Billy

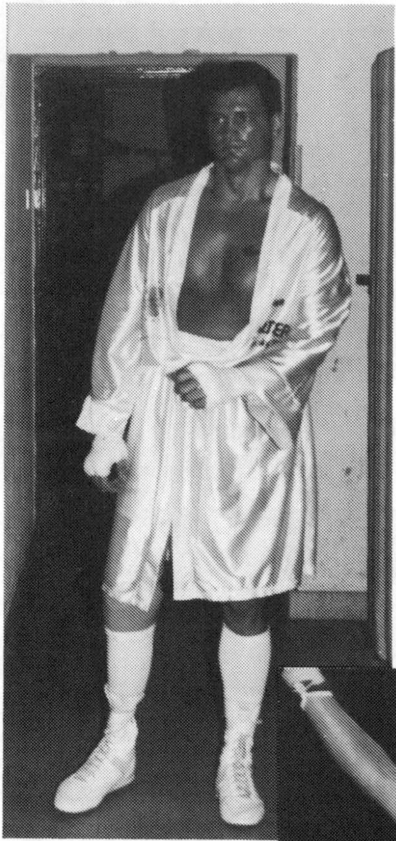

Rehearsing the fight plan for an upcoming battle.

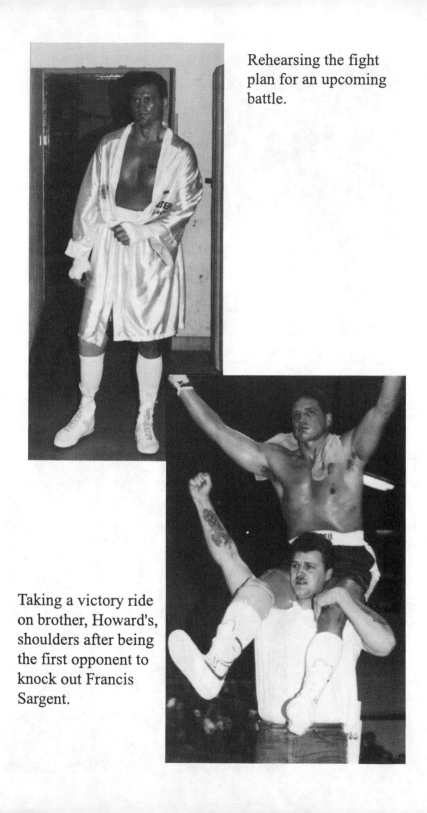

Taking a victory ride on brother, Howard's, shoulders after being the first opponent to knock out Francis Sargent.

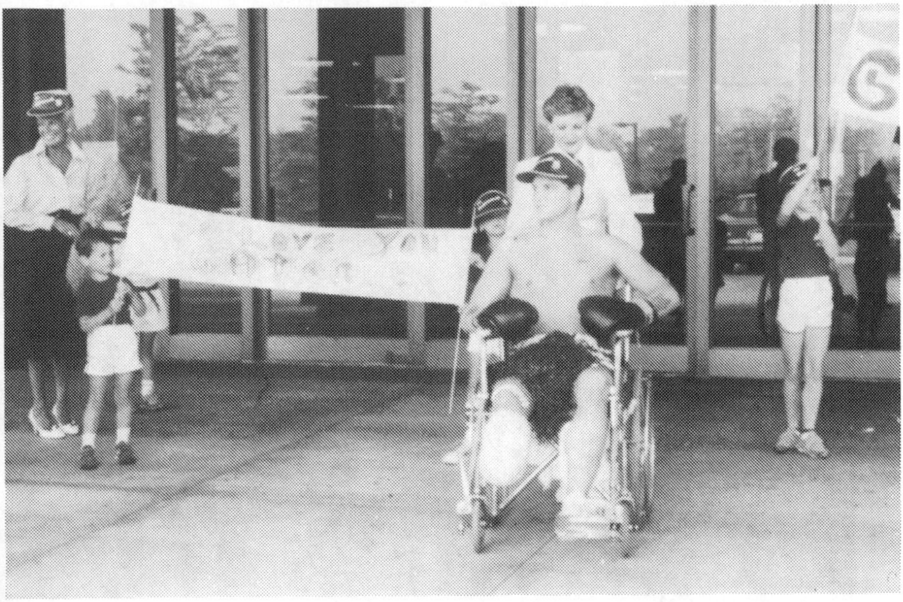

The "Gator" is wheeled out of the hospital following his amputation.

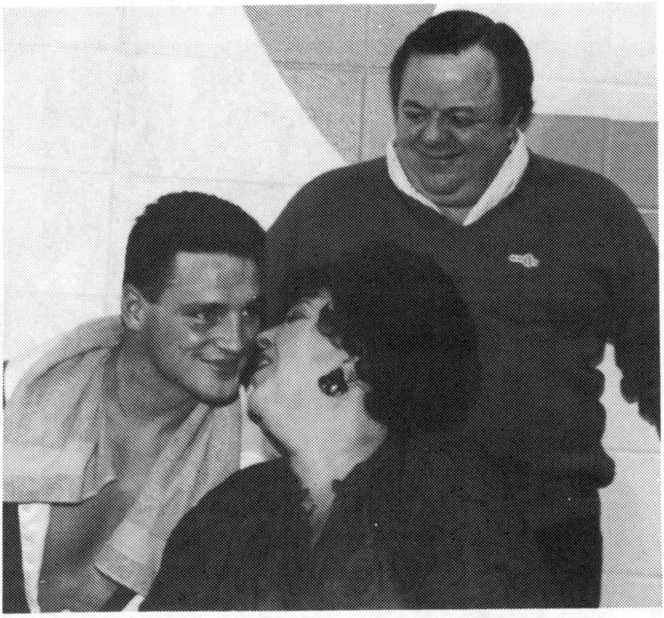

A kiss for Mom, his favorite lady, with manager, Jerry Lenza looking on.

Taking in a few words from his mentor, Mr. O'Conner.

Early professional days. Getting ready for a knockout.

Put up your dukes, Don King! Craig and his promoter, King, discussing a potential fight against Alfonzo Ratliff.

Two black eyes and two titles following victory over Anthony Witherspoon.

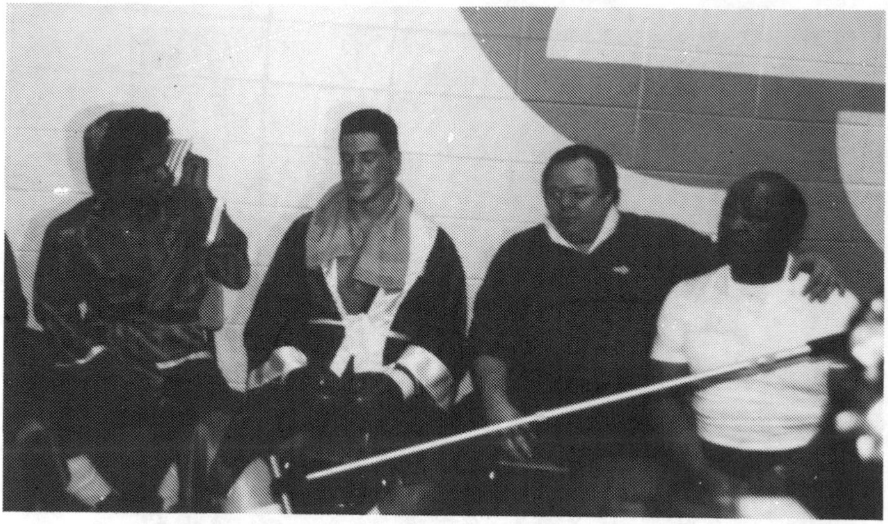

Post fight press conference after the Francis Sargent fiasco. Jerry and trainer, Nate Bolden, looking on.

Squaring off with Pope John Paul II at a papel audience in Rome.

Hamming it up with the NFL's greatest running back, Walter Payton.

Craig, "the Gator", in his favorite pose.

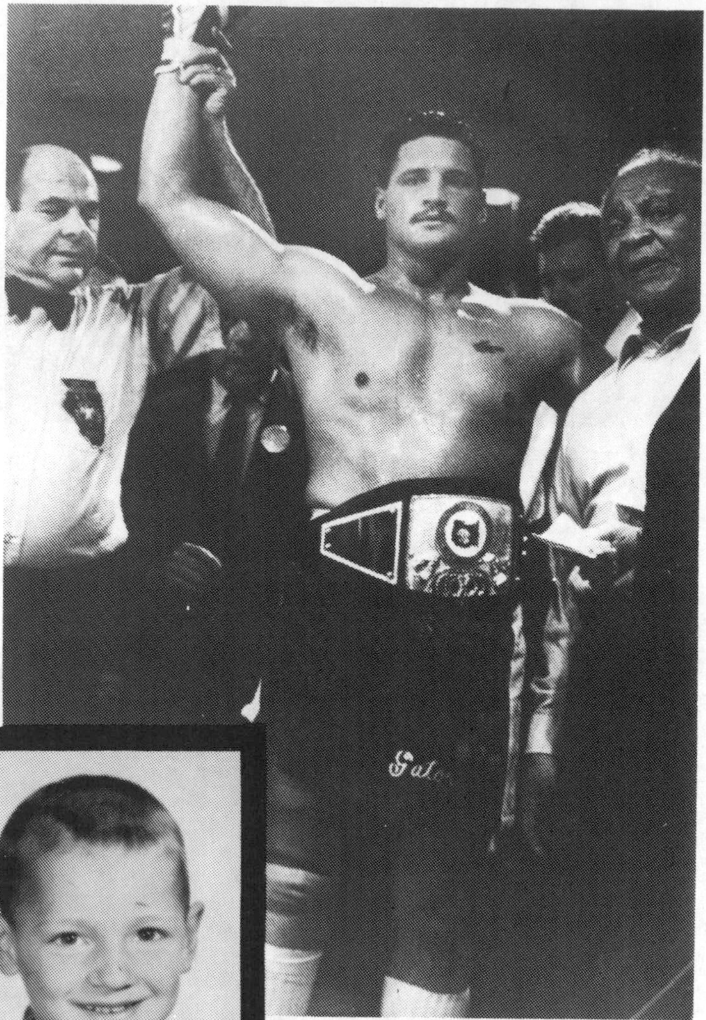

Claiming the Illinois State Heavyweight title with trainer, Nate Bolden, at his side.

A photo that prove's Craig didn't spend every minute of school in the principle's office.

Hamming it up with Father Clements of Holy Angels Catholic Church who arranged a charity boxing card. Craig scored a knockout in this exhibition which featured Mike Tyson.

Two lovely members of the "Gator" fan club.

TEN

I was making good progress in the gym, but it was getting hard to stay focused under the constant scrutiny of the media and curiosity seekers. Getting in quality workouts was becoming a problem with all this new attention coming my way. I needed to be able to concentrate on ways to improve as a boxer. I wanted to prove I was a contender, not a sideshow attraction.

An opportunity to achieve that end came my way early in the summer of '85. Jerry had a friend with a large building for sale in the southwest suburb of Hickory Hills. We grabbed it, and took pride in opening my first "Gator's Gym." We had boxing and weightlifting facilities. In what little spare time I had, I instructed club members on the basics of boxing. The operation became successful. I even sold plenty of Gator memorabilia in a concession area. For my own training purposes, I usually went to Fuller Park or Woodlawn Park in the ghettoland. That's where the top-flight sparring partners were. Meanwhile, the people interested in gawking at me were looking around my new place in the suburbs.

At Fuller Park, former old-time boxers from Nate's era ran the show. Arthur Moore, a religious old-timer, dedicated his life to training boxers for God. He claimed to once have a piece of Sonny Liston, when the former heavyweight champion lived in Chicago. Arthur was the first coach of Oliver McCall. Sadly, by the time McCall was making millions as heavyweight champion, Arthur had long been forgotten. But, he made a real difference in the lives of hundreds of inner-city amateur boxers. After a workout I liked to hang around and shoot the bull with the old-timers. Herman Mills, another of Nate's cronies, also trained boxers there. Herman was inducted by Mayor Daley into the Chicago Senior Citizens' Hall of Fame. He had participated in almost one hundred professional fights, but you sure couldn't tell by looking at him. Herman had been a classic defensive wizard. He once dropped a close decision to legendary former world featherweight champion, Willie Pep. Herman had supplemented his ring earnings by working as a tap dancer. We used to spend hours together in front of the mirror working on my footwork. Herman showed me all the moves. If I never fought again, at least I could be one hell of a tap dancer. I'll never forget the advice Herman gave me about knowing when to hang up the gloves for good. There are three signs to look for: first your legs go, then your reflexes go, and finally your friends go. Talk about kidding on the square. More than one great fighter has left the sport blind and broke. My hopes were to turn my misfortune into a fortune.

Advice from these well-seasoned ring veterans was always welcome. To show my appreciation I gave Herman and Arthur some venison I had scored on a successful hunt. Neither one had ever eaten venison before, and I thought they would enjoy this tasty wild game. When I handed over the wrapped meat, Herman and Arthur both looked at me funny. Only after I assured them it was good eating did they dare take it home. They were amazed I was an expert with the rifle. The only gun shots they were familiar with were those heard in the neighborhood surrounding the gym. I gave them instructions on how to cook the venison. Next time I saw them they begged for more. I became known as the "Deer Hunter" around the gym.

It's hard to believe, but my movement in the ring was actually better than it had been with two flesh-and-blood legs. I know it sounds impossible, but it's true. Before the accident, I never concentrated on my footwork. I relied on my solid chin and offensive skills to keep me out of danger. Now, with a prothsesis, I worked night and day to improve my mobility. I always wore sweat pants at the gym to avoid drawing attention to my new foot. When reporters came to see me, I liked to give them a hard time. Sometimes they couldn't remember which leg I had amputated, and I'd make them guess. I felt great when they chose the wrong one.

Eventually their constant presence started to wear on me again. It seemed to me that I fielded the same stupid questions day in and day out. I understood their interest, up to a point, but I felt I should be treated like a rising contender, not the freak du jour. Finally, Jerry came up with a solution.

Jerry Lenza: *"Carmen Graziano was one of the best trainers in professional boxing. He had played an instrumental part in Joey Giardello* *winning the middleweight title back in 1963 and had been training contenders ever since. He was helping with John Collins' training duties as well as with rising contenders like Carl "The Truth" Williams, Dave Tiberi, and Kip Kane. Carmen was in Williams' corner the night he lost a highly disputed decision to Larry Holmes. Carmen invited Craig to come out to New Jersey and stay at his secluded training camp."*

Getting out of town was a terrific idea. Carmen Graziano was the complete opposite of Nate, and it took some time to get used to the difference. He looked like an Italian Rodney Dangerfield and was extremely outspoken and opinionated. He could be confusing and insightful at the same time. He was full of one-liners. One of my personal favorites was: "Potential unrealized equals zero." It made sense.

I will never forget the first time I saw Carmen in New Jersey. John Collins, his long-time trainer, Tony Arvia, and I shared an apartment in Jersey. Graziano stopped by on our first night in town to make sure we were settled in. We were sitting around watching television when he knocked on the door. His first words were, "Where is Bodzianowski?" When I stepped forward, Carmen said, "Show me what you got, Bodzianowski!" I asked him to wait a few minutes until I got my leg on. Forget the leg, he said and start shadow-boxing now. I tried to explain that I needed my leg for any type of boxing, but he was adamant. So I hopped around on one leg throwing the best combinations I could. My swings didn't have too much behind them; I was too busy trying to keep my balance. Carmen seemed a bit frustrated. I tried not to let it bother me. I knew I would prove myself to him in the gym the next day. Little did I know the surprise in store for both of us then.

> **Dave Tiberi: (former middleweight title contender)** *"Carmen initially felt we would have to treat Craig with kid gloves, but that is the last thing you do with a guy like Craig Bodzianowski. Craig surprised all of us with his optimism."*

I arrived at the gym wearing my most-worn prosthesis. I had already broken a few other ones, and wanted to see how much punishment the device could take. I figured the first day at the gym would be light workouts anyway. I loosened up by shadow-boxing for a few rounds and then was gloved-up to spar. I hadn't sparred since my injury, and was expecting a light session. I would be working with Kip Kane, a big heavyweight who had lost only once in about twenty fights. They were grooming Kane for a bout against "Neon" Leon Spinks who was once again trying to capture lost glory in his roller coaster ring career. If Kane got by Spinks, he would get a shot at Larry Holmes's world title.

The bell sounded for the first round of our sparring session. I came out moving, flicking out soft jabs. The only ring work I had done in the last year was shadowboxing, and I planned to work on my timing and get a feel for the ring. Kane had a different plan. He came charging at me like a bull with smoke steaming from his nostrils. I retreated to the ropes, covering up and picking off his shots with my shoulders and gloves. Every punch Kane threw had KO written on it. After about thirty seconds, I started firing back with my own artillery. I slipped one of Kane's right hands and countered with a left hook that dropped Kane as if he had been shot by a cannonball. As he rolled around the canvas, I saw Graziano out of the corner of my eye. His jaw was about touching the ground and his eyes almost popped out of his head. His hot-shot prospect had been knocked on his ass. This was my domain and no one was going to take this opportunity from me.

Jerry Lenza: *"Carmen did not tell Kip about Craig's leg. And he sent Kip right after him."*

To this day, I am not sure why Carmen, God rest his soul, sent Kip Kane after me like that. I wonder if he thought I did not belong in boxing anymore and he wanted Kane to kick my ass to get me the hell out of the sport. Maybe it was his way of testing me to see what I had. I guess I will never know.

They raised Kane, and our next three rounds were less frantic. Carmen instructed us to hold the power punches for the next few rounds. In the fourth round, Kane got another shock when my prosthesis snapped in two. It made a loud noise and then fell apart. Kane freaked out. He had no idea I had a fake leg. Fortunately, Mike Quigley had given me an emergency number in Philadelphia to get a replacement. Within twenty-four hours my leg was fixed. Once again, it was Quigley to the rescue.

Upon completion of our sparring contest, Carmen was full of compliments. "I have never seen anything like this," he said. "There was no limp and you had excellent mobility. Your left hook was wicked. I have been involved in boxing for over forty years and if I hadn't seen this for myself, no one could have gotten me to believe it. If you have any problems getting sanctioned by any boxing commission, I'll go to bat for you." We hit it off really well after that. You had to respect the guy. He had once been a naval officer and had graduated from Villanova with honors. Now he was coaching world-class fighters.

However, for all his smarts, I would not let him change my boxing style even though he complained a lot about my left jab. He claimed I didn't bring it back to the proper defensive position after delivering it. Though I respected the man, I wasn't changing my style for anyone.

Training in New Jersey benefited me in many ways. Nobody knew who the hell I was out there which let me concentrate solely on boxing. I worked out with Kane more, and had him use his weight advantage to lean on me and try to push me around and manhandle me in every way. I wanted to be prepared for anything.

Since my injury, two Chicago boxers had won titles—Alfonzo Ratliff and LeeRoy Murphy. Both were in my weight class. Only in boxing can you have more than one guy claiming to be world champion in the same division. The sport is ruled by numerous separate governing bodies. More titles mean more money to them and the promoters. Ratliff had recently claimed the World Boxing Council (WBC) cruiserweight title with a decision over Carlos DeLeon. LeeRoy Murphy knocked out Marvin Camel in his own backyard to claim the International Boxing Federation (IBF) cruiserweight belt. Boxing's other major governing body was the World Boxing Association (WBA) which recognized its own champion. It was rare for one fighter to simultaneously hold all three major belts. Although Ratliff and Murphy called themselves world champions, in my mind they weren't even the best cruiserweights in Chicago as long as I had a leg to stand on. All I needed was the chance to prove it.

Meanwhile, Carmen ran a tight ship at Archer's Gym in Pleasantville, New Jersey. His boxers lived in a smelly old house near the gym. Curfew was at 10 p.m., and morning roadwork was at six o'clock sharp. As good as it was to be away from Chicago, I would not wish those Spartan conditions on anyone. There wasn't a woman within miles.

My one-time amateur foe, Carl "The Truth" Williams, was also in camp. He hadn't gotten any friendlier since we last met. When we saw each other again, we exchanged aloof grunts and Williams mumbled, "I remember fighting you in New York. You were the only amateur I couldn't knock out."

"You still can't knock me out!" I told him. I didn't care if he was now a top heavyweight contender.

On one of my last days in the Garden State, I sat down with Carmen. He was behind me one hundred percent by then, but confided that it had not always been the case. "When I heard you were coming out here, I looked up your record in the 'RING Record Book & Encyclopedia'," he said. "It listed your entire career results, but in parenthesis it said you retired after losing your foot. Frankly, I didn't think it possible for you to continue boxing. Was I ever wrong!" I appreciated Carmen's endorsement. He had been a difficult guy to win over.

I hardly gave my prosthesis a second thought anymore. It was almost as much a part of me as the real thing. If I accidentally kicked something with my artificial right foot, I even yelled "Ouch!" I returned to Chicago ready to prove to the Illinois State Athletic Commission that I deserved a professional boxing license.

Jerry Lenza: *"The Illinois State Athletic Commission was under serious national scrutiny. They had the media and several other state boxing commissions breathing down their backs. Some members of the commission had not appreciated Craig before he lost his leg. However, the Illinois*

State Athletic Commission always treated Craig fair. In October of 1985, I notified the five-member board of the Illinois State Athletic Commission that Craig would be reapplying for his license."

There was no way in hell they could deny me a license. I had just held my own with some top contenders on the East Coast and was prepared for any test the commission had in store. If they didn't give me a license, then no other boxer in the state deserved one either.

Frank Glienna (Chairman of the Illinois Boxing Commission): *"The commission took a very negative look at the situation at first. I was concerned about how he would obtain leverage with his prosthetic foot. It did not seem possible for him to compete at first, but we owed Craig the opportunity to state his case."*

The first test was to spar in front of the commission. I'm not sure what they expected, but what they saw was a much-improved boxer. One of the board members, Dr. Glenn Bynum, was attending physician at most Chicago-area fight cards. I knew he was against my comeback. *Sports Illustrated* quoted him as saying I might not be mobile enough to avoid punches.

But I had support in the medical community too. Dr. Michael Treister, an orthopedic surgeon who had served as a ringside doctor for over ten years, expressed no trepidation about my prosthesis in an actual bout. A boxer who suffered numerous knockouts in the ring was at much greater risk than me, he said. That went for someone with a neck injury or torn rotator cuff, too.

My own orthopedic surgeon, Dr. Robert Eilers, also cast a vote for me on the grounds it was unfair to deprive me of the opportunity I had worked so hard to achieve.

Outside the ring I was already living as if the accident never happened. I led my softball team in hitting and slid into bases both head first or leg first, depending on the situation. I drove a stick-shift truck and bicycled ninety miles a week. I even got my time down to 6:02 in the mile run. (The newspaper reported that I could run a mile in less than six minutes, but unless the cops were chasing my ass, I wasn't quite that fast. But I could sprint at nearly 20 miles per hour.)

Finally, judgment day arrived. I had done everything in my power, and now everything was in the hands of the boxing commission. Jerry phoned with the good news. I had my license to box again.

> **Frank Glienna:** *"The commission received approval in writing from several orthopedic surgeons. They convinced the commission Craig could make a comeback. Craig worked so much harder now after the accident. I felt no matter what happened, the accident was no longer a factor in his career. If the medical specialists said it was not detrimental to his health, who was I to say it was?"*

I wanted to come back with a bang, and told Jerry to book Francis Sargent for my first bout. Sargent had been my most difficult fight. While I was off, he had been active the past year-and-a-half, and most recently had posted a unanimous decision over Jerry Harris. Sargent had never been stopped, and if I knocked him out my comeback would be regarded as the real McCoy. Conversely, if I didn't do well against him, I'd know myself I was finished. Fighting some tomato can would prove nothing.

ELEVEN

My return to the ring was scheduled for December 14, 1985, at Alan Shepard High School in the nearby suburb of Palos Heights, Illinois. A high school gymnasium was a unique location for a professional boxing show. I liked the fact that it was close to home, because I would know just about everyone there.

> **Jerry Lenza:** *"Cedric Kushner was in charge of the promotion and we wanted an affordable location near Craig's neighborhood. We had to give Sargent an inflated payday. He knew how bad we wanted him as an opponent. Craig also received the best payday of his life. I wanted Craig to make some money because I still was not sure what would happen with his career. We sold out the fight within days."*

The media attention surpassed my wildest imagination. Dick Shaap of ABC News came out to interview me and to watch me train. Shaap was the author of one of my all-time favorite quotes. After promoter, Don King, was acquitted on fraud charges, Shaap said that "King's reputation took a terrible pounding. He was found innocent!" ABC broadcast my interview on national television. After the interview, Shaap had asked me to join him on a trip to the airport to pick up a special friend coming in for a movie shoot. I was curious about the identity of the mystery guest. I even offered to drive.

I noticed Dick glancing at my legs as I operated my stick-shift truck. At a red light, he asked, "Craig, how long does it take you to put on and take off your prosthetic leg?"

"I can take this leg off, smack you over the head with it, and have it back on before the light turns green," I proudly answered. His opened-mouthed grin showed that he obviously enjoyed my response.

Shaap's friend was none other than actor-comedian, Billy Crystal. He was in town to film the adventure comedy *Running Scared*. I was amazed at how much he knew about the fight game. He asked to attend my afternoon workout at Woodlawn Park and I warned him about the dangerous area surrounding the gym. It wasn't exactly a movie sound stage he'd be going to.

Billy took a long look around the broken-down neighborhood around Woodlawn Park. Some panhandlers near the gym had no idea who Crystal was as we passed on our way to the gym. They gave the normal "What's up, Gator?" but didn't even take a second look at one of Hollywood's biggest stars. I think Billy actually enjoyed being anonymous. He asked a lot of questions about my training methods. I offered him tickets to my fight, but he was scheduled to leave town the day of the bout. It wasn't every day a real movie star attended one of my workouts, and it was a pleasure to meet Billy Crystal.

Three days before the fight, my pal, Mike Moe, phoned early in the morning with excitement in his voice. "Gator, did you see today's *USA Today* yet?" he asked.

"No, I just came back from a morning run and now I'm headed back to bed," I said.

"Check out the sports section Gator, there is a picture of us working out together," Moe stated in excitement. I promised to read the article but instead headed back to bed. It was always nice to be written about in the paper, but Moe was beside himself now with his fifteen minutes of fame. I was amused by his enthusiasm. My own thoughts remained focused on the big event just a few days away.

Preparation is the key to success, and I was never more ready for anything in my life. We even practiced putting on a new prosthesis in the corner just in case something happened to my artificial leg during the fight. We covered all the contingencies we could think of, including getting my fake foot trampled on either accidentally or on purpose. We needed to be ready for all situations.

The media supported my comeback for the most part. A reporter from the *Philadelphia Daily News* wrote that I seemed to have little power on my right side. My response was if I had trouble planting to throw my right hand, I hoped I always had that problem. My right hand packed as much punch as it always had, but my left hook was now even more dangerous.

Boxing historian, Herb Goldman, of *The Ring* magazine, said mine would be the first professional boxing match ever involving a man with a missing limb. Several boxers have competed minus toes or fingers, but a one-legged boxer was unheard of. Making the "Guinness Book of World Records" had never been a life's goal, but what the hell.

> **Jerry Lenza:** *"There were days when this kid was in tremendous pain, but he was not going to show anyone how much he hurt. On several occasions I told him he needed to talk about his pain. Craig never used the accident as an excuse, although there were plenty of times he could have. Finally all of his hard work was going to pay off."*

My last day of training was my best ever. I ran my fastest mile. I sparred sixteen rounds, and my combination punching had never been better. I couldn't wait for the fight.

I arrived early at Shepard High and I listened to music as Nate wrapped my hands and discussed our strategy. Well-wishers streamed into my locker room, but I wasn't very sociable. My mind was already in the ring. Tonight was the night I was proving I was back. I wanted to win impressively. If I became the first guy to knock out Sargeant, that would make a loud statement to the boxing world. There'd been talk a good showing could lead to an appearance on the nationally televised *Good Morning, America* show.

The undercard bouts moved along at a rapid pace. Chicago-based boxers, Jeff McCracken, James Dixon, and Jimmy Valleyfield all scored victories. IBF cruiserweight champion, LeeRoy Murphy, and John Collins boxed a fast-paced three-round exhibition. After a brief intermission, I was summoned to the ring.

The small gym was packed. The atmosphere was electric, and my favorite song, "Bad to the Bone," was blaring in the background. I rested my hands on my brother Howard's massive shoulders as I made my way in to the ring behind him through a sea of fans. As I climbed through the ropes the crowd noise achieved an even higher volume level, and somehow grew louder still during my introduction. I couldn't even hear my name announced. But then the place got eerily quiet, as if someone had flicked off the switch, when I took off my shiny red robe. I could feel everyone staring at my leg. A moment later the switch was flicked on again, and the decibel-level was incredible.

Cedric Kushner grabbed the microphone and thanked everyone in the crowd for attending. Then the introduction of my opponent followed. Francis Sargent received a polite applause that was quickly obliterated by the loudest "Gator! Gator!" chant I had ever heard. I was so moved by it, I even felt goose bumps forming on my prosthesis!

We met at ring center for referee, Stanley Berg's, instructions. Finally the moment of truth had arrived. I stood patiently in my corner waiting for the opening bell.

At the bell, I shuffled to ring center. The prosthesis was in working order just as it had been in hundreds of rounds of sparring. I popped out a few jabs at Sargent, just feeling out the situation. As expected, he got on his toes and began to run. I moved to my right to cut off the ring. Sargent did not want to mix it up. He moved side-to-side, avoiding danger at all cost. He must've thought that by moving around he was taking advantage of my weakness. But my own ring movement was now better than ever. It can be difficult to look impressive against a guy who doesn't want to fight, but I never stopped pressing Sargent and started to sting him with left jabs. Midway through the round, I caught him with a one-two combination. Sargent continued to run but I knew the fast pace would soon affect him. Near the end of the round, I nailed him with a looping overhand right and followed with a series of left hooks to the body. I could hear the crowd scream each time I landed a punch. The bell sounded to end the opening round as I confidently walked back to my corner. A first round knockout would have made a hell of a statement, but I was actually hoping to go a few rounds to test my prosthesis in actual competition. Besides, a first-round knockout would have deprived me of one of life's greatest pleasures... the ring card girl.

I stood in my corner between rounds as Nate splashed water all over me and passed on instructions for round two. I could not help but notice the gorgeous brunette ring card girl who strutted past my corner during the end of the sixty-second intermission. All thoughts quickly reverted back to the fight plan. I would have plenty of time to concentrate on the opposite sex after the fight.

Sargent resumed running his ass off when the bell started the second round. I knew it was only a matter of time until I caught him. I slipped several of his jabs, stepped in and returned a left of my own. When Sargent snapped my head back with a jab, I realized the track meet was over. He wanted to fight all of a sudden, which put us on equal footing. I dug left hooks into his midsection, then landed a hard right and two left hooks that rocked Sargent. His eyes rolled back as he slumped to the canvas. I stood in a neutral corner as the referee began his count. The place was in a frenzy as Stanley Berg's count tolled "8...9...10." I raised my arms in the air and reveled in the moment. Nate was the first to reach me. My brother, Howard, then hoisted me on his shoulders for a victory lap. I felt incredibly happy and fulfilled. I was a contender again, marching on two strong legs toward a shot at the world title.

At the press conference afterwards, I dedicated my victory to all the people who stopped believing in themselves after a large set-back or handicap. If I could make it back, it might inspire other handicapped people to believe they could do something meaningful with their lives. If I would have listened to all the doubters I would still be in a hospital bed, or out drinking somewhere.

Gloria Bodzianowski: *"I cried in sadness when I first heard about the accident, but tonight my tears were full of joy."*

I celebrated with a pizza. It tasted a hell of a lot better than tuna and potatoes. All the emotion surrounding my comeback left me exhausted. I wanted to sleep in the next morning, but was awakened far too early by my excited mother.

Good Morning, America was on the phone. It was arranged for me to fly to New York in two days to appear on the show. Jerry lined up dinner plans with Cedric Kushner in New York the night before we were to be on the show. Francis Sargent was also invited to appear. The day before I left for the Big Apple, I made arrangements for a rare night on the town with some friends. I needed to let off some steam after the months of training I had recently been through. I phoned Hillbilly and Mike Moe, and we planned to hit the town hard.

It felt great to have an ice-cold beer in my hand. It had been too long. My mistake was not sticking to beer. As we hopped from tavern to tavern we started doing some shots. I had never been good with shots, and this night was no different. We got so loaded, I have no idea how we even made it home.

In the morning I was awakened by a familiar loud and extremely unpleasant sound. The old man was mad as hell. He was pacing up-and-down the hallway yelling at the top of his lungs, "Why me? I do not deserve this! Son-of-a-bitch, somebody is going to pay for this!" I was only half-awake but my head was now pounding from the high rate of alcohol consumption the previous evening. My first thought was that we had crashed into Dad's brand new truck when we got home in the wee hours of last night. Dad's voice grew louder as he cursed and stomped up and down the hallway. It did my throbbing head no good.

Finally, I snapped. As much as I loved my old man, I was ready to rumble with him. I put on my leg and jumped out of bed, then opened my bedroom door slowly and cocked my fist, ready to feed him a right hand before he could punch me. "What's up, Dad?" I asked in a deceptively non-confrontational way.

He looked at me with smoke coming out of his ears and yelled, "Son-of-a-bitch! Your Grandma just got here!" Whew! I wiped away the sweat that had just broken out on my forehead.

"That's it, Grandma's here?" I asked. He just nodded. You could say my old man and his mother-in-law had a love/hate relationship. Most times the old man loved to hate Grandma. I was relieved to head for New York the next day.

The *Good Morning, America* people put us up in one of the ritziest hotels I had ever seen. The place was well over $500 a night. A whopping amount, and close to what I earned in my first professional fight.

Cedric Kushner took Jerry and me to a fancy downtown restaurant. We made it an early night in order to be rested up for my first live national TV appearance. It would be great exposure, and could only help my comeback.

Host, David Hartman started the segment by airing a brief clip of my knockout of Sargent. Then Hartman turned to Sargent himself, sitting there with us on the set, and asked for his evaluation of what we'd just seen. Sargent was very complimentary towards me. He told Hartman that nothing seemed to be missing from my repertoire. My balance and ability to cut off the ring were superb, said the guy who was in a better position than anybody but me to know. Sure he was a bit overwhelmed fighting in my backyard, Sargent said, but he had given his best effort, holding nothing back. As far as my future in boxing was concerned, I would go as far as my will and desire took me. There wasn't much I could add to that. Sargent acted with class the whole time we were on the air, and I really respected him for it. But if I'd known what was waiting for me back home, I would have kicked his sorry ass again right there on national television.

"I THREW THE FIGHT" blared the front-page headline in the December 22nd, *Chicago Sun Times*. The story quoted Sargent as confessing that he took a dive against me!

Where the hell did that come from? We'd just spent a couple of days with the guy in New York, and Sargent never said anything even remotely like that. In fact, he'd gone out of his way to tell the whole country that I'd beaten him fair and square. But now, according to the newspaper, the fight was just a swindle, rigged to make me look good. Sargent claimed that he felt threatened by the mostly-white crowd, and that he'd gotten harassing calls leading up to the bout. For weeks, he said his wife would answer their phone and hear racist epithets.

I told the papers I was all for an investigation of the fight, but that it had better include a lie-detector test for Sargent. I'd take one, too. "Fix", my ass! I'd nailed that son-of-a-bitch with a punch that not only put him down but also raised a lump on his face as big as a golf ball. If what happened to Sargent was phony, so was World War II.

Of course my response was dutifully noted in the press, but given most people's cynicism about boxing anyway, it would take more than that to dispel the new cloud hanging over my career. It pissed me off, because I had worked so damn hard, and done everything by the numbers. I knew what was really behind it all—prejudice against the handicapped. It's people who have both legs and still can't make anything of their own lives who have a hard time admitting a one-legged man can do anything.

Jack Cowen (International match-maker based out of Chicago): *"I booked every one of Craig's bouts. Sargent lost the fight fairly. The fact that one writer at the* Sun Times *put the story on the front page blew everything out of proportion. If the article had never been featured in the daily paper, little would have been made of the situation."*

When his shit hit the fan, Sargent attempted to apologize, claiming he had been misunderstood. All he meant to say was that he "blew the fight." Sargent claimed he was scared and confused during the newspaper interview. Until I made him a big name by punching out his lights, nobody ever noticed Sargent before. He was just a journeyman, unused to the attention he had suddenly received. He said he was quoted out of context. He later claimed to say he threw the fight away by letting the crowd psychologically affect him. It was reported that Sargent had a minor history of freezing in big fights.

Jerry Lenza: *"I accepted Sargent's apology, but I did not accept excuses that put him in a position where he had to apologize. I do not believe Sargent took a dive. Craig defeated him outright. But, Sargent's comments took something away from the victory, which was unfair to Craig."*

Cedric Kushner was outraged, and recommended that Sargent be banned for life. His theory was that Sargent had difficulty admitting defeat to a one-legged fighter. Even Sargent's manager, Jerry Moore, believed a full investigation would prove that Sargent legitimately lost. Moore told the press that Sargent could hardly talk before the fight, he was so nervous. He was worried about the crowd, not the fight.

If you review the tape of our fight, you'll see Sargent knocked to the canvas and then clutching his eye as he tries to get back to his feet. He almost did beat the count, but it didn't happen. Neither did anything else other than the fact that Sargent got his clock cleaned. A brief lapse in concentration over concern of the eye injury cost him valuable seconds as he attempted to beat the count. Sargent quit because he was hurt and could not reach his feet by the count of ten. That is a hell of a lot different than quitting because he was paid. Sargent should have admitted defeat like a man.

Jerry Lenza: *"The alleged fight-fixing scandal was yet another obstacle for Craig to overcome. Craig had already resumed his ring* *career after an eighteen month absence due to amputation. This accomplishment should have been the entire focus following the Sargent bout, nothing else. This scandal was the last thing we ever dreamed of or wanted to happen. Unfortunately, it took away from Craig's fine effort. It was unfair. If Craig ever gets beat, he will not make excuses."*

I just wanted to move on with my career. I know that I'll always have doubters, but they can't beat me. My goal was to get ranked and then get a title shot. Good riddance to all the controversy. I told Jerry to get me another fight as soon as possible against a quality opponent. So he placed this tongue-in-cheek advertisement for one in the Sun Times:

HELP WANTED: BOXING
One-legged cruiserweight, Craig Bodzianowski (14-0), needs opponent who is experienced 10-round fighter weighing 205 pounds or less. No experience in fighting one-legged boxer necessary. But request applicant be willing to fight his best and accept outcome without excuses. Pay is negotiable. Last applicant earned $1,200 but, to everybody's embarrassment, claimed he faked second-round knockout because of death threats. Applicant should contact Jerry Lenza at 312-555-5570.

We played the media game, too.

TWELVE

Christmas Day was almost here. Our whole household had put the holiday on hold until the completion of the Sargent fight. My mom did her best to spark some interest for Christmas Day. "Craig," she joked, "What do you want Santa to get you for Christmas?"

"A new leg," I told her honestly.

I had been working out with two different synthetic feet. I had the 'Seattle Foot' against Sargent, but had been training with an even more modern version of the 'Flex Foot.' It was lighter in weight and had a bit more spring to it. I could move around better and run easier with the new model. I had run two miles each morning testing it. In between my early roadwork and afternoon gym sessions, I went pheasant hunting and walked up to twelve miles tracking those elusive birds. I also sparred and jumped rope with the Flex Foot. For all its advantages, the trouble was it was not really as durable as the Seattle Foot. I broke more than a few Flex Foots, and at over $6,000 a pop, it got a little expensive. Fortunately, Mike Quigley and Oakbrook Prosthetics were helping with my expenses.

The media frenzy was crazier now than ever. I was flooded with interview requests from all over the world—Stockholm, Paris, and Rome to name a few. I was flattered by all the attention but I did not want to interrupt my training schedule for a trip abroad. I was awfully tempted though, especially when an acquaintance told me every woman in Sweden was a gorgeous blonde. It sounded like some sort of Utopia but the timing was not right. I had plenty of media requests in the United States to deal with. Most of my press attention was positive, but then boxing's famed "Fight Doctor," Ferdie Pacheco, decided to stick my foot in his mouth.

On February 2, 1986, *NBC Sports World* televised 1984 Olympic Gold medalist, Meldrick Taylor's, tenth professional fight. After Taylor's victory, the network aired a 15-minute segment on my comeback. Reporter, Dorothy Lucy, compared me to that wondrous fighting machine, Rocky Balboa. They showed a picture of my friends carrying me out of the hospital and film of me running in the freezing cold weather and working out at the gym. They even went to our house, showing a clip of the entire family. My seven-year-old nephew Jeffry made the most of his brief air time. He jumped up and hurled punches in the air. It was still too early to determine if we had a prospect in our midst! NBC then followed me to the gym filming my workout. My pal Sargent was on, too, making the most of his fifteen minutes of notoriety. This time he admitted the legitimacy of our fight. I wish the thing would have ended there, but then they went back live to ringside to give Pacheco his say.

The man some people in boxing sneeringly refer to as the "Fright Doctor" knocked the Illinois commission for letting me fight. If I got hurt, Pacheco said, there would be a vast outcry to abolish boxing. In fact, he added, he might be the one to lead the charge.

Now, everybody is entitled to his own opinion, but you'd think someone trained as a physician would be interested in checking out my case history before questioning my fitness to pursue my dream. I had never met the man. To begin with, I had lost a leg, not an arm, and therefore could as the referee says, protect myself at all times in the ring. Secondly, I had already passed a stern medical examination. If Pacheco would have done his homework, he wouldn't have talked so loosely. I wonder if he even watched the segment on me that preceded his blast. Didn't he hear Frank Glienna state that I had been reinstated only after the commission conducted extensive medical examinations which I passed, and that he was confident the risk to me was no greater than any other professional fighter?

The topsy-turvy reception I was receiving in Chicago went beyond anything I could fathom. However, by February I grew tired of the freezing weather. On most days I returned home from my morning run with icicles stuck in my exposed hair. When Jerry invited me to train in Las Vegas for the next six weeks, I jumped at the chance. John Collins was scheduled to face contender, Robbie Sims, in March in Las Vegas, and I was going to be training with him.

Carmen Graziano was in charge of our camp. He put John and me together in a hotel room with a young prospect named Dave Tiberi. Dave was fresh out of high school and had just made his professional debut a few weeks earlier. He was a polite, religious kid who didn't cuss. John and I instantly took this naive kid under our wings. One day we went checking out the local stores. We stopped in one across the street from the hotel. It was a music store run by a set of beautiful African-American twins. We questioned the gorgeous twins on where to go for a good time. Dave wondered about the well-lit nightclub down the street. The sisters said it was a gay bar often frequented by Liberace. "Davey, let us know what you think of the place," I joked as everyone laughed in approval. John, Dave, and I continually pulled pranks on each other. It helped make training bearable.

We trained daily at the Golden Gloves Gym, a converted airplane hanger with two rings and plenty of space for the large number of boxers constantly training there. Some of the world's best fighters trained there, including future light heavyweight champion, Virgil Hill, and James "Black Gold" Shuler. Shuler was an undefeated middleweight preparing to take on multi-division champ Thomas "Hit Man" Hearns. Poor Shuler. Hearns stopped him in the first round, and just days later Shuler was killed in a motorcycle accident. It was quite a reality check; it made my motorcycle accident seem minor in comparison.

I sparred often with Tiberi to prepare him for his second professional bout, scheduled for the Collins / Sims undercard. I had almost 30 pounds on Dave, and so I pulled my punches and worked on my timing.

Dave Tiberi: ***"Carmen Graziano instructed me that members of the Nevada Boxing Commission would be on hand for our sparring session. He said to just stay inside on Craig and work on slipping punches."***

The first few rounds went off as planned. In our third round sparring I went to Tiberi's body with a left hook then followed up with another hook to his head. Tiberi left his face totally exposed and my punch landed with much more force than originally intended. Dave staggered back and his eyes rolled up in their sockets. But, after a brief rest he insisted on continuing. The gutsy kid even worked a few more rounds with another boxer after we finished. Little did I know that my powerful punch to Tiberi's head would come back to haunt me. Tiberi suffered a delayed reaction type of amnesia from the punch and unintentionally got even with me later.

When we were done working out, Tiberi headed back to our place while I checked out some sights on the strip. When I returned to our pad, Tiberi was acting out of character. He informed me I had received a phone call from my girlfriend. "Did you get her name?" I asked in somewhat of a disgusted tone. Fortunately, I had a good idea who phoned. Later on in the evening, I tried to get more information out of Tiberi but it was to no avail. When we returned after dinner, I phoned my current girlfriend. Luckily my intuition was correct, but she wondered who the drunk was that took her call earlier. "What did he actually say to you?" I questioned.

"He told me you were across the street at the gay bar with Liberace," she responded. I could only laugh when I heard that. It turned out that Tiberi had suffered a mild concussion from the left hook I landed in our sparring session. Luckily, within days Tiberi was back to normal and resumed training again for his match with Canadian amateur champion, "Danny Boy" Lindstrom. Lindstrom was at least ten pounds heavier than Tiberi, and a heavy favorite. Tiberi only got the fight because Lindstrom's original opponent backed out at the last minute.

Carmen Graziano stuffed Dave at breakfast the day of the fight to add some poundage by the weigh-in. A bloated Tiberi finally hit the scales at 165 pounds. Danny Boy

Lindstrom had to sit in the sauna in order to come in at the contracted maximum weight of 175 pounds. I grabbed a ringside seat at Caesar's Palace to watch my two friends fight in an evening that produced mixed results.

Tiberi was slated to box in the swing bout, which meant it had no definite spot on the card. It would be set at the promoters' discretion. Dave put on a brilliant display of boxing, holding Lindstrom to a six-round draw. Having seen first-hand Dave's exceptional skills and heart, it came as no surprise that he eventually challenged for the middleweight title.

Tiberi boxed circles around champion, James "Lights Out" Toney, but the three blind mice judging the bout somehow scored Toney the winner. Dave was so disgusted he never fought again. He even wrote a book titled "The Uncrowned Champion" voicing his take on the fight.

> **Dave Tiberi:** *"To be involved in Craig's life was so special. Many people feel there is a certain darkness to boxing, but a guy like Craig shined a bright star on the sport. He was extremely optimistic. Craig was a great motivator who led by example. In gym workouts, Craig was always trying to encourage everyone else. It was the opposite of what you would expect; you would have thought everyone should have been encouraging him. Initially, Carmen Graziano brought Craig to New Jersey and Las Vegas as a great motivator, but he soon realized Craig was world championship material."*

I wish my friend, Collins, would have done as well in the nationally televised main event as Tiberi had earlier in the evening. Collins never got on track, and was hammered to the canvas three times by Sims in the first round for a devastating TKO defeat. John never fought again. As hard as it was to watch John go out that way, the bright lights and big-fight atmosphere fueled my desire to be a champion. I returned home more determined than ever, and once again found a big surprise waiting for me.

> **Jerry Lenza:** "*I received a call from an agent representing a new program in Italy titled "Italia Sera." The show was hosted by popular young actress Maria Theresa Ruta, and focused on people involved in unusual circumstances. I was a little leery at first due to the negative comments voiced by Ferdie Pacheco on the NBC segment. I did not want Craig to be put in that position again. Finally, after a right of first refusal was signed guaranteeing us the ability to censor the script for the telecast, I consented. Craig did not need me to protect him. He always handled himself well with the media. This time he needed me because I wanted to go to Italy more than he did.*"

When Jerry told me, he was so excited I barely understood him. Jerry was a devout Catholic of Italian descent. There was really nothing about Italy that excited me. The language was different and I couldn't read the menus. And worse, terrorists had made several recent hits in that part of the world. I told Jerry to tell them, no thanks! I could sense his disappointment when I declined the offer, but Jerry was not so quick to give in.

The next day, he said the Italians had substantially increased their offer. It sounded more tempting, but once more I declined. Jerry wasn't about to concede defeat without a fight. "Craig, is there anything that can be done to get you to accept their generous offer?" he asked.

I told him, "If you can arrange for me to meet the Pope, I'll hop on the next plane." Fat chance, right? Don't ask me how it happened, but the next day two round-trip tickets, that included an audience with His Holiness at the Vatican City, landed on my doorstep. We headed for Rome on February 10, 1986, three days after my twenty-fifth birthday.

Up to that point, my only international experience had been fishing in Canada. Rome had once been the cultural center of Europe. I fell right in love with Rome—especially the local cuisine. The food for the most part was simple with a bountiful taste. Since Italy is almost entirely surrounded by water, seafood, a favorite of mine, was plentiful. And pasta, of course, is almost the official national food. It came in all shapes and sizes, covered with sauces of every description. Since I wasn't fighting again for two months, I ate everything I could get my hands on. After a tour of the town, Jerry and I headed in for an early night. I wanted to be rested for my international television debut.

The host of *Italia Sera*, Maria Theresa Ruta, looked stunning on film and even better in real life. I was taken aback by her beauty right away. A popular actress in Italy, she was starting her own talk show there, and had handpicked me to be a guest on it.

There were two other panelists. One was a Sylvester Stallone look-alike who even came on the show dressed in full "Rocky" attire. He and I did a photo shoot together at a gym in downtown Rome a few days after the show. The second guy was actually a pygmy straight out of the African bush. I had seen this bewildered little fellow that morning at the hotel, looking scared and confused. He freaked out coming down the escalator. This was only his second day in so-called civilization. An anthropologist spotted him in the jungle. I swear the pygmy had two left feet! In all my years, I never thought I would be sharing the spotlight with a pygmy and a Stallone want to be!

On the show, they aired highlights of my victory over Sargent, then flashed a picture of Mike Moe and me working out at Gator's Gym. Unfortunately the piece was not aired back home. The exposure would have been nice for the gym. Maria Theresa then asked me questions about my accident and comeback. I fielded her concerns under difficult circumstances. First of all, every question and response had to be done through an interpreter. It was important to get the question correct the first time so you didn't come off as an idiot. Secondly, it was hard to concentrate because Maria Theresa was so damn gorgeous. I had a difficult time keeping my eyes off her. Maria Theresa even made me bare the Gator tattoo on the air. I was so smitten, I probably would have bared anything she wanted.

After the live broadcast I suggested to Jerry that we invite our hostess to dinner. Jerry picked out a restaurant, and also invited along a translator and some employees of the hotel. I was glad the translator came along, otherwise I would have had a difficult time conversing with the blonde bombshell.

> **Jerry Lenza:** *"Eight of us packed into a small car and headed for a popular pizza place on the outskirts of Rome. We were practically on top of each other in the small vehicle. Craig managed to stay awfully close to Maria Theresa. I could hear Craig attempting his best pick-up lines through the interpreter."*

After dinner we all headed back to the hotel bar for a few cocktails. As the evening progressed, I noticed my Italian had improved dramatically. Just before midnight, I kicked Jerry under the table and gave him a quick wink. He understood, and excused himself. Unfortunately, so did Maria Theresa a while later before calling it a night. My first night in Italy had been quite memorable, but it couldn't hold a candle to what was ahead.

Jerry Lenza: *"The Pope gave a special Mass on the second Wednesday of each month. The one we attended fell on Ash Wednesday. We had to pick up our tickets for the church service inside the Vatican. Once we arrived, we went to the Gates of St. Anna. We walked through these huge glass double doors then headed down a long beautiful marble stairway. Finally, we climbed a large flight of stairs until we reached Archbishop Marsinkus's office. The Archbishop acted as the right hand man for the Pope. 'Gator is that you? Are you there?' It was Archbishop Marsinkus speaking from behind his office door. He then came out to greet us. He was a large athletic man in his early 60s. He was from Cicero, Illinois, on the outskirts of Chicago. He looked at Craig and said, 'You are the Gator Man. I have heard all about you and have been looking forward to seeing you.' Then he looked at me and said, 'Lenza, huh? Did you ever know a man named Hippo Lenza who ran a classy restaurant in Chicago called Club-El-Bianco?' I told him Hippo was my father. 'Great restaurant,' he said. 'I have eaten there many times.'"*

Archbishop Marsinkus handed us two large colorful tickets for the church service. They had the letters “VIP” stamped on them and resembled Super Bowl tickets in size and texture. As a show of thanks, we invited the Archbishop to dinner but he kindly declined. Then we headed off to the chapel.

We entered the small chapel located next to the beautiful ancient cathedral. At the door we were met by well-dressed guards carrying large bayonets. One of them looked at our tickets and commented that we must be very important. He spoke perfect English and later confessed he was from Detroit.

The guard walked us right up to the front row of the filled-to-capacity church. To our left sat a group of nuns, on the right was a young priest and his ailing mother. It was the closest I had ever come to a truly religious experience. I had attended church on an irregular basis, but nothing compared to this. I tried to remember the last time I had attended Confession, and the word ‘never’ came to mind.

> **Jerry Lenza:** *“I introduced myself to the young priest seated next to us. He had once worked in Rome for the Pope. His mother was terminally ill and she was here for a final blessing from the Pope.”*

Bright lights appeared and the Pope descended from an entrance beneath the ground. Everyone applauded and the Pope greeted us in several different languages. He made his way around to the VIP section. He greeted the dying elderly woman and blessed her. When it was Jerry’s turn, he looked nervous and bent down and kissed the Pope’s ring. I had never seen him so excited in my life. The Pope made his way to me. He smiled upon his initial greeting. He was one of the few people who pronounced my last name correct on the first shot. He laughed, reminding me that he was from Poland. He put his hands in the air and said, "Put 'em up, Gator." I took my boxer's stance and squared off against the head of the Catholic Church. Cameras flashed everywhere. The Pope then blessed me and wished me continued success in my career. A sensational feeling shot through my whole body. It made me feel as if I could conquer the world.

Jerry Lenza: *"The entire experience brought tears to my eyes. Craig also seemed extremely touched by the whole affair. When my family and friends witnessed the pictures of me and the Pope, they got quite misty eyed. The Catholic Church has always meant so much to us.*

"Upon exiting the church, several people recognized Craig from the television show the previous evening. For the remainder of our stay in Italy, Craig was noticed wherever we went. People would yell 'Gator' in broken English in restaurants, stores, or when we were walking down the street. Craig was hounded for autographs, but he didn't seem to mind."

I was amused to see the picture of the Pope and I squaring off in the paper the next morning. Before boarding the plane home, we visited the Sistine Chapel, famous for its wonderful masterpieces created by Michelangelo. I guess a little culture never hurt anyone.

The four days' stay in Italy was a vacation I needed before I went back into serious training. It had been rewarding for the mind and soul. I was not far from peak condition. Notwithstanding, I did have a pound or two to lose from all the good Italian cuisine I had been feasting on.

THIRTEEN

My April 6th fight against Ric Enis would be televised live on USA Cable network. I knew some of the so-called experts were still calling my comeback a hoax, but I didn't let it affect me. People can only intimidate you as much as you let them.

Enis had a respectable record of fourteen victories against seven defeats. All of his wins were by knockout. In his last effort, Enis was knocked out for the first time ever by WBA cruiserweight champion, Dwight Muhammad Qawi. I heard Enis was an exceptional athlete who had once been an All-Big-Ten fullback at the University of Indiana. Playing football for Indiana gave him plenty of opportunities to taste defeat. I planned to feed him another loss.

A capacity crowd filled the Americana Congress Hotel in downtown Chicago for the Enis match. Al Albert and Randy Gordon called the fight live for the USA network. Gordon would soon be appointed commissioner for the

New York State Athletic Commission. He'd been quoted as saying, "Bodzianowski's comeback is truly the stuff that Hollywood scripts are made of." That was nice, but then he went a little overboard with the movie allusions, saying that even when I had two feet I moved like Frankenstein. Gordon claimed I had never been a Hector "Macho" Camacho type speedster before the accident. Gordon was trying to be complimentary as he continued claiming my ring movement had enhanced magnificently after the accident. Gordon attributed my improvement as a testimony to the human spirit. I appreciated the excellent publicity, but knew if I did not defeat Enis impressively, all the positive press I had been receiving would come to a screeching halt.

I rehearsed my game plan many times as I sat in my dressing room waiting to be called. Nate reminded me of the importance of respecting Enis's much heralded power. I meditated while I awaited my nationally televised debut. Finally, I made my way to the ring. Once again I was led into the ring by Howard, with Nate and Mike Moe trailing close behind. I could feel the overhead lights beating down as I waited for the introductions. Enis was announced first and received brief, polite applause. I was overwhelmed by the roar that filled the arena when it was my turn. The hometown crowd's energy gave me a tremendous boost. Enis would have to knock me senseless to stop me. Little did I know how close he would come to doing just that.

Nate told me to respect Enis's power, so I chose to box at the beginning. I pumped a few lefts in his face and traded shots on the inside. Enis then connected with a powerful uppercut that I felt from head-to-toe. I returned a looping overhand right as he was coming in. Whenever Enis came close, I dug left hooks to his mid-section.

I started the second round up on my toes, circling and peppering Enis with jabs. Enis was trying to land a single bomb to end the fight and he was reaching me with an occasional punch. My left eye began to swell. Enis landed one below the belt and was warned by referee, Stanley Berg. In retaliation, I started winging left hooks. One made Enis stumble into the ropes. As I was closing in, Enis threw an overhand right that landed flush on my jaw. My brain momentarily short-circuited as I staggered into the ropes. With 10 seconds left in the round, Enis caught me with another overhand right, and threw some left hooks to my body. One of the latter ventured south of the belt line again, and Enis lost a point for the foul. It was his head punches that had me in trouble when the bell sounded to end the round.

My handlers worked desperately to revive me during the 60-second interval. Enis knew I was still shaky and came out swinging in the third. I grabbed him for a quick breather, but he shook me off and started firing again. I stumbled around like a drunk exiting a tavern on Bourbon Street. Nate was standing and yelling from the ring apron, and the referee told him to sit down. I backed against the ropes and applied a cross-arm defense, picking off most of Enis's onslaught with my elbows and shoulders. As hurt as I was, I was still aware enough to know an opportunity when I saw one. It came when Enis left himself wide open after a punch. I slammed a counter left hook hard against his exposed face and he crashed to the canvas. He was no Sargent. He got up and I caught him with a perfectly thrown overhand right that knocked him down, leaving his head resting on the bottom rope. He didn't move while the referee counted 10.

Nate was the first one in the ring to greet me. I had begun to notice that Nate's mental condition was growing worse by the day. He had a hard time dealing with the heavy amount of leather Enis had landed on me in the second and third round. Nate was becoming too emotional during my bouts. I am sure his advancing age had something to do with it. He also suffered from high blood pressure. I feared he might actually have a stroke or heart attack at one of my matches. Fortunately, Nate understood the risks involved and agreed to bring in some assistants to handle the workload. Meanwhile my celebration continued at ring center.

Announcer, Albert, called it a miracle comeback, adding, "Sylvester Stallone could not have scripted it better." As satisfying as it was, I knew I needed to be more impressive to be viewed as a legit contender—instead of boxing's greatest (and only) one-legged fighter.

> **Jerry Lenza:** *"We had a difficult time booking quality opponents for Craig. We tried to book a name opponent like former 175-pound king, Matthew Saad Muhammad, who was making a comeback at cruiserweight. But the fight fell through. Most boxers felt that taking on Craig was a no-win proposition. If they won, they accomplished little because they only beat a one-legged fighter. On the other hand, they feared what could happen to their reputation by losing to him. Many people also realized beating Craig would be an unlikely task."*

I was next scheduled to fight on June 23rd as part of a live professional boxing card in Chicago preceding the closed-circuit telecast of a Las Vegas fight card featuring Thomas Hearns, Roberto Duran, and Barry McGuigan in separate bouts. However, I developed an infection in my right stump that kept me from wearing my prosthesis for several weeks, and the bout was rescheduled for August 10th. The sight was the parking lot of Jerry's restaurant, Artie G's, in Palos Heights, with Steve Mormino in the other corner.

> **Jerry Lenza:** *"We marketed the 1,600 seat location as "The Caesar's Palace" of the Midwest. The ring was situated in the parking lot using a natural incline. There was not a bad seat in the place. We hired our own private security company to aid the Palos Heights police in running the affair smoothly. It's always risky holding an event outdoors, but we had a rain date set up just in case. Craig was thrilled with the outdoor location. It was only two miles from his home, and most of his neighborhood would be in attendance."*

The outdoor location suited me fine. I was especially glad there would not be all the cigarette smoke that always seemed to fill the indoor fight locations. I was crazy about any activity that took place outdoors. I spent lots of nights before this bout fishing for big mouth bass and blue gills in a nearby private pond. It provided good peace of mind. After the Mormino bout I wanted to plan a boar hunting trip, but first I had to take care of business. The boxing experts were finally starting to notice me as something more than an oddity. I broke into the international rankings when the WBC listed me as the number 30 cruiserweight. It was recognition a long time coming, and I couldn't afford a misstep now by thinking about anything besides Mormino. He was a rugged club fighter out of St.

Louis, who had just out-pointed my last victim, Ric Enis, and was now determined to bag himself a Gator.

> **Steve Mormino:** *"At first I did not want to fight Bodzianowski. I felt it was a no-win situation boxing against the guy with only one leg. But, I had just lost my job and needed the money to support my family. It was a decent payday and if I defeated him, I would be in line for even better paydays. I had tremendous admiration for Bodzianowski continuing to box after the accident. But if he connected with one solid shot, I aimed to forget all about the one-legged stuff, and he would be in serious trouble."*

The S.O.B. gave me a hell of a fight. I never hit anybody with so many punches before without knocking him out. Mormino made me miss a lot, too, with fluid upper body movement. I won a unanimous decision by a wide margin, and was glad the fight went the entire eight-round distance. I needed the work, and it also reassured me that my prosthesis could handle a long contest. Now I wanted one more bout before I took on a rated contender.

In addition to achieving success in the ring, a goal of mine was to prove to handicapped people everywhere that with hard work and a positive attitude, life could progress in a meaningful way despite physical setbacks. My comeback was also a two-pronged benefit to the manufacturers of my artificial foot. It gave them a ton of free advertising and tested their product to the limit. A handicap is no laughing matter, of course; but part of getting beyond something is learning not to take it too seriously. I didn't.

A charity in the suburbs held a parade in my honor. Everyone was supposed to dress in a costume. I offered to come as a pirate with a red parrot on my shoulder and my own authentic peg-leg. Another time, I was shopping for new shoes, when the clerk suggested I try on the right mate of the one he'd already chosen for my left foot. I quickly unfastened my leg when his back was turned. When he turned back around I tossed him my artificial leg and joked, "You put this one on while I tie up my left one." His eyes almost popped out of his head.

In the gym once, I was pumping iron when a 25-pound weight crashed down on my synthetic foot. A guy lifting a few feet away came racing over to help, thinking my foot had been shattered for sure. I convinced him that if it had not been for the expensive, custom-made protective shoes I had on, that would have been the case. Then I dropped a 45-pound weight on my prosthetic foot to prove my point. The excited weight-lifter said he once had been seriously injured when a falling weight fell on his foot, and offered me $100 right there for my crummy, ordinary shoes. My laughter killed the deal and I pulled up my pants leg to show my artificial foot.

Jerry wasn't thrilled when I rejoined my softball team. He feared I'd break my good leg or bust myself up sliding into a base head first. But the worst thing that happened occurred when I was wearing an older prosthesis that needed a serious tune-up. The bolt fastening the foot to the leg was constantly coming loose. My first time at bat, I took a mighty swing at an inviting pitch. I hit the ball hard, but my foot came undone as I spun, and I ended up doing a complete 360° turn before falling on my ass. The funny thing was, the foot part of my prosthesis remained stationary the entire time. To the uninitiated, like the umpire who started yelling "Call 911" at the top of his lungs, it looked like I had done something that usually happens only in cartoons. Meanwhile, I jumped up and gimped toward first base.

My next fight was for the title. The Illinois state heavyweight championship, that is. The opponent was Chicago heavyweight, Bobby Hitz. Hitz was a natural heavyweight, but a far less experienced fighter. He had a record of 8-0 and was known as a straight-in slugger. The vacant Illinois State Heavyweight Title would also be on the line. Unfortunately, it was not a world championship, but it was a title of sorts none the less.

> **Jerry Lenza:** *"Name boxers still wanted no part of Craig. There must be a certain stigma attached to facing a one-legged fighter. It was that handicapped business all over again; as if Craig had not proved the prosthesis was not a disadvantage. It was starting to get frustrating to still be overlooked by the contenders. Craig was in the best condition of his life for the Hitz encounter."*

My first recollection of Hitz goes all the way back to the Golden Gloves. He lost in the finals to Oliver McCall. Now I planned to hand him his first defeat as a professional. I was promised a match with a ranked contender if I was victorious against Hitz in impressive fashion.

Hitz and I were well familiar with one another. We had crossed paths in the gym and I had attended a few of his professional contests. He was being groomed as an unbeaten up-and-coming white heavyweight. His real name was Robert Hitzleberger, which did not conjure up the image of a tough heavyweight, but his fighting name was now Bobby "The Hit Man" Hitz. My goal was to temporarily turn him into the "Horizontal Man" for our match. Hitz declared that my name would look good on his boxing record. In my opinion, a loss would not look good on his record, but I would be happy to fight him.

The event was staged at the large banquet hall, Condesa Del Mar, in the south Chicago suburb of Alsip. We were the ten-round headliner of an eight bout card. Two former world heavyweight champions, Ernie Terrell and 'Smokin' Joe Frazier, would be in attendance. Frazier was in town to be a cornerman for his protégé, Oliver McCall, and his son, Tyrone. The facility was sold-out well in advance.

Hitz promised that he would come out punching. I am happy to declare that Bobby Hitz is a man of his word. He came out like a sprinter in the 100-yard dash. Meanwhile, I paced myself looking for weaknesses. Hitz had never gone past four rounds so I figured he would tire early. Hitz threw a lot of leather in my direction, but near the end of the round I thumped him with a left hook that was a sign of things to come. On paper Hitz won the first round but it did not matter because I planned to make it an early night.

Hitz and I stood toe-to-toe throughout round two. My combination punching was scoring continuously. Hitz had no shortage of guts and gamely fired back, but I was reaching him oftener with a higher volume of punches. A perfectly executed left hook dumped Hitz on his ass. Courageously, he beat the count right before the bell.

Bobby came out dancing in the third round, a sign that he had enough of the close-quarters combat. No problem. I cut off the ring on him and a devastating left hook sent Hitz down. The gutsy "Hit Man" got up again, but, I swarmed all over him and the contest was halted by referee, Stanley Berg.

. Hitz begged for an immediate rematch and told the press he should have moved and boxed more, but I feel that would have only prolonged his agony. After retiring a few years after our bout, Hitz began promoting quality monthly professional cards in the Chicagoland area. He also owns an Italian restaurant, Nana's Café, in downtown Chicago next to Harry Carry's.

> **Bobby Hitz**: *"I really thought I was going to beat Craig Bodzianowski. Looking back on it, Craig had too much experience for me. He beat me fair and square, but he would never grant me a rematch. George Foreman and Craig Bodzianowski were the only two guys I ever really wanted to fight again. As my career progressed, I improved a lot as a boxer and wanted to redeem myself against those two."*

> **Ernie Terrell (former world heavyweight champion):** *"Hitz-Bodzianowski was fun while it lasted. To me, Craig is already a world champion. He got cut down in his prime but he would not let the leg amputation stop him. Personally, I do not know how anybody can top what he has done. I have never seen anybody so determined in my life."*

I was now officially the baddest heavyweight in Illinois. The state title didn't carry much weight, but the belt still felt good around my waist, which was bigger than usual. I had gained almost fifteen pounds to fight as a heavyweight. When reporters teased me about the excess,

I reminded them that Muhammad Ali didn't always have a washboard stomach either.

I felt like the Rodney Dangerfield of boxing. Ex-heavyweight champ, George Foreman, had recently announced he was going to give boxing one more shot at age thirty-seven. He had been inactive for nearly ten years. He tentatively signed to fight Bobby Hitz in Sacramento, California, on March 9th, but Hitz was denied a license by the California boxing commission. Promoter, Don Chargin, explained that the commission felt that if Hitz had another 10-rounder under his belt he might be okay. But his only 10-rounder was against the one-legged guy, and he got knocked out. They didn't want to reward that. I let comments like that roll off my back. Years later, Hitz received his dream bout with Foreman and was promptly splattered in one round.

Bobby Hitz unanimously decisioned Mike Tyson on March 25,1988. Who said Hitz never fought any name opponents! Yet, this Tyson resembled "Iron Mike" in name only. He hailed from Iowa and sported a not so lofty record of 2-5 going into the Hitz fight. He was quoted in the newspaper as saying his friends identified him as the "b.s.Tyson".

The "b.s.Tyson" once fought in California and was notified that there was a warrant out for his arrest. The police had been checking with the California boxing commission. It turned out he was mistaken for the heavyweight champion who was accused of slapping a security parking attendant. The "b.s. Tyson" almost took the rap. If only he could fight like the real Tyson. Rumors were surfacing that he might not even have been the toughest Mike Tyson in Iowa!

It was time for me to box a ranked contender. It had been thirty-one months since the accident. I had won four consecutive efforts and felt ready to pick it up a notch. Offers poured in from all over the world, but I preferred to stay at home. I liked fighting in my backyard and my paydays were increasing with each bout. I sold a lot of tickets every time I fought, and I had a notion that a civil war with my old friend, Alfonzo Ratliff, would sell out any facility we chose.

Ratliff had recently dropped his world title to Bernard Benton and was now under contract to Don King. He also just moved up to heavyweight. I always believe in setting high goals, but fighting "Iron Mike"Tyson in his first heavyweight fight may have been pushing it. After lasting just two rounds with Tyson, Ratliff promptly dropped back down to cruiserweight. Now he was available, which made two of us.

FOURTEEN

Carlos DeLeon was the WBC cruiserweight title-holder, and Evander "The Real Deal" Holyfield was the WBA ruler. If I defeated Ratliff, my next fight could be worth millions. Cedric Kushner had formed a working agreement with Don King. King's son, Carl, was the manager of record for Ratliff, but the man with the electric hair-do called the shots. "Only in America" said King senior, employing his trademark phrase, could a man with one leg earn a shot at the world title. King invited me down to his hotel room as soon as he arrived in Chicago for the fight. King was never one short of words and he filled my head with lucrative promises if I defeated Ratliff.

I had been warned about Don King. A famous story summed up his *modus operandi.* When 'Smokin' Joe Frazier defended his world title against George Foreman in 1973, King accompanied Frazier to the stadium. After Frazier had been knocked out, King consciously left with his new best friend, George Foreman! So I was wary of a celebrated con when we met as soon as he got to Chicago. I listened though, because when Don King talked there was always the sound of cash registers in the background.

Not that they had opened very much for Ratliff. Currently rated number 9 by the WBA, he had been inactive for almost eight months since the Tyson debacle. Ratliff's turbulent relationship with Don and Carl King had been well documented. He had only seen $20,000 of his official purse of $75,000 for squaring off against the then-current heavyweight champion. Ratliff felt overlooked and exploited. He now viewed himself as a pawn in King's massive stable of fighters. A victory over me was his only chance to revitalize his career. A loss would effectively end it.

> **Alfonzo Ratliff:** *"If I lost this fight I knew I would be facing the 9-to-5 working world. I was initially hurt by the loss to Mike Tyson but afterward I reasoned 'who hasn't been beaten by Tyson?' Bodzianowski had made a remarkable comeback, and if he defeated me he deserved a world title shot. But that would not happen. This represented a long overdue opportunity to fight in my hometown. For me to be defeated by Bodzianowski, they would have to carry me out of the arena on a stretcher. Bodzianowski was the nuttiest guy I had ever sparred with. He always kept coming no matter what I caught him with. I was prepared for a war."*

It had been several years since Ratliff and I had sparred. Back then Ratliff was an established contender and I only had a few professional bouts. He was the king of the hill at Woodlawn Boxing Club at that time. I did not follow his progress very closely. I knew he had won the world title and had since fought Tyson. I never watched televised matches. I was a fighter, not a fan.

> **Jerry Lenza:** *"We felt it was time to make our move with Craig. The match with Ratliff would be an excellent chance to see where we were as compared to the rest of the division. Ratliff had only lost to guys who at one time or other were either heavyweight or cruiserweight champions. Ratliff gave both Pinklon Thomas and Tim Witherspoon tough times before losing. If Craig got past Ratliff, a world title bid was the next step."*

The ballroom of the Bismarck Hotel was sold out on April 12, 1987. Ratliff was the first to enter the ring. I made him wait before I made my entrance. The idea was to let him prowl around under the bright lights and burn energy. I also wanted to give him time to think about the fight and get antsy. When I finally left my dressing room, I noticed 'Gator' banners hanging from the rafters. Friends and well-wishers reached out as I walked to the ring with Howard, Nate, and Tom Fornarelli.

From the ring Cedric Kushner introduced Ernie Terrell, John Collins, and LeeRoy Murphy. Then, with great enthusiasm, he introduced Don King, who was greeted by the crowd with noticably less enthusiasm. I felt bad for the guy sitting directly behind King. How the hell was he going to see the fight over that light-socket-hairdo? The Illinois state cruiserweight title was at stake—I had worked hard to get back down to 190 again—but the belt wasn't needed to dress up the promotion. Howard went over and watched Ratliff glove-up in the ring. Not that we did not trust Ratliff, but no need to take any chances with a fight of this magnitude. Finally the referee called us to ring center, discussed the rules, and then instructed us to come out fighting.

I charged out aggressively, pawing with my jab to measure my distance. Ratliff was moving side-to-side. Ratliff landed a lead left hook followed by a right hand as I was coming off the rope. He held a definite advantage in reach and intended to use it. After I popped him with a few jabs, Ratliff turned aggressor and opened up with both hands as I covered up along the ropes. I was uncharacteristically tight, and Ratliff took advantage of that. But we started trading heavy leather on even terms. I could hear the crowd volume rise each time I landed a punch. Ratliff kept trying to score with his favorite punch, the right uppercut, so I wasn't looking for it when a left uppercut snapped my head back and sent me crashing flat on my back. My head hit the mat with a resounding thud and felt as if I was in some type of dreamland as I worked myself up to a sitting position only to go crashing face-first back down. It's funny about getting whacked like that. It doesn't really hurt, but has more of a stunning effect, sort of like having a hundred flash bulbs go off in your face at the same time.

I managed to narrowly beat the count, but was still quite out of it when the referee waved us on to continue. Ratliff jumped all over me and I covered up. The bell ending the round was a big relief. Nate jumped in the ring and escorted me back to the corner. In spite of my handlers' expert efforts to revive me, I remained so stunned that to this day I can't recollect anything about the next three rounds. I needed to look at the fight tapes to later see what followed.

At the bell I somehow darted out right after Ratliff. He clinched and backed me up against the ropes and began firing away. I managed to slip or catch most of his bombs and finally got my jab working again, snapping it in Ratliff's face. The tide turned as I spun Ratliff around to the ropes and punched away. I threw a succession of left hooks and uppercuts that tagged him. The action moved to ring center where we continued to trade power shots. I started getting the better of our exchanges. I pursued Ratliff right to the bell. It was a brutal give-and-take round, but I clearly won it. At the bell everyone in the place was in a frenzy. It was a hell of a better scene than the tomb-like one which filled the auditorium at the conclusion of the first round. I must've felt good myself, because I even stood between rounds!

I hammered out jabs and made Ratliff miss with many of his punches in the third. But then he didn't miss with a left hook that got my attention. Our pace was slowing, but I managed to work Ratliff against the ropes and land a few damaging left hooks. Again I had him reeling on the ropes from solid shots. I was getting stronger, while Ratliff appeared to tire. I stayed on him until the bell. I confidently made my way back to the corner. The crowd was going berserk. Don King's electric hair was even hard to detect in the excitement.

Ratliff and I lobbed bombs throughout the fourth round. I was stepping in with thudding jabs that jerked his head back. But Alfonzo answered back each time. It was a close round but it seemed I did enough to win it.

My first recollection of the fight after the knockdown in round one, is of the ring card girl walking around before the fifth round. I'm still not sure if it was her string bikini or the bucket of ice dumped down my shorts that brought me around. The taxing brawl had taken a toll on both of us. That's when you find out who has guts and has paid his dues in the gym. I pumped my fists in the air between rounds to Jack up the crowd even more. I could taste the world title shot promised to me if I won this fight.

Ratliff started loading up on his blows, trying to throw a Hail Mary shot. I landed a picture perfect four-punch-combination that shook him, and he answered with a hard straight right and sizzling left hook. We went toe-to-toe till the end of the round.

For the first six rounds, we battered each other senseless. I had gone six rounds before, but never at such a fatiguing pace. Enis had me momentarily stunned in our bout, and Mormino went the distance without returning much punishment. This time was different. Ratliff was providing me with the biggest test I had ever faced in the ring. The leg was not even an issue. Between rounds Nate instructed me to keep it up. He felt I was winning the fight with only four rounds left to go.

Going into the seventh round, I had a slight lead. Sensing he was behind, Ratliff came out strong in the seventh. I kept sticking jabs in his face. We were each landing a high percentage of shots. Near the end of the round, Ratliff battered me against the ropes to make it close, but I raised my arms in victory to the crowd's approval as I headed back to my corner.

Every time I was hit, I instinctively returned a counter shot. So did Ratliff but I thought I took the eighth. Apparently the crowd agreed: the "Gator, Gator" chant filled the hall. It was another close round. Nate told me between rounds that I was only six minutes away from my title shot. I felt comfortably ahead as I made my way out for the ninth round.

Both my eyes were bruised and swollen as I lifted myself off my stool to tread into the uncharted waters of the ninth round. Ratliff came out desperately swinging, knowing he needed a miracle to pull out the fight. He pinned me against the ropes and fired an eight-punch combination topped off by a left hook that knocked me on my ass. I jumped up quickly, and Ratliff continued to bomb away. Although weary, I dug deep and came up with a seven-punch combination that sent Ratliff stumbling into my corner. But I knew the knockdown would cost me dearly on the scorecards. In pro boxing, the guy who's knocked down in a round usually loses it on the scorecards by a 10-8 margin. According to professional ranks, a knockdown is scored as a point. Most rounds are only decided by single point, so in essence it was like I lost two rounds. I'd been down twice, and even though I'd come roaring back I knew the fight was extremely close. My corner thought I held a slight edge, but instructed me to win the last round.

In the tenth, the math really went against me, thanks to another looping overhand right that landed flush on the button. I took a few steps, then tumbled to the canvas. It went in the books as another knockdown, but it was more from weariness than anything else. I sprang up quickly. Ratliff jumped on me. I let it all hang out, looking for the knockout. I backed Ratliff in the corner and opened up with both hands. I stalked Ratliff relentlessly, attempting to land one mighty right to end the fight. Each time I landed, he stumbled. He was gushing blood from his mouth and had cuts around both eyes. I pursued him right to the final bell. When it rang the crowd gave us a standing ovation. Ratliff came over and we hugged.

I knew the last two rounds cost me dearly, but I still felt I would win, and when the announcer declared the decision was unanimous I threw my hands up in the air in victory. But all three judges saw it the other way. Tim

Adams scored it 46-45 for Ratliff, but had the rounds even. Judge Jerry Jakubco had it 46-43, and had it 5-4-1 in rounds. The final judge, Bill Lerch, scored it 47-42, and 6-3-1 in rounds.

Alfonzo Ratliff: *"Bodzianowski gave me more hell inside the ring than anyone else ever has, including Mike Tyson. The shots I was hitting Craig with, he had no business getting up from. He got up and fought back as if he was possessed by demons. Tyson's punches were quick, but Craig's were more of a punishing blow. You can never take a guy with that type of determination for granted. I had never suffered so much physically from one fight. I'm still mad at him for the way he made my face look that night".*

Jerry Lenza: *"Looking back on it, we may have jumped the gun on the Ratliff fight. Since the Sargent fiasco, the media had been clamoring for Craig to fight a contender. Craig also wanted the fight. At the time we still were not sure how many more fights Craig could condition himself for. Although he will never admit it, stamina-wise the training was notably taxing. He had never faced a guy of Ratliff's caliber. The fight represented a great opportunity which we felt was worth taking."*

My first professional loss hurt in more ways than I can express. If I had won, my next fight would have been for the world title. I had come so close to climbing the mountain and to fall off now was sickening. I ached physically and emotionally. Several people suggested I pack it in. As for Don King, he was nowhere to be found.

The day after the fight I was awakened by a telephone call from Jerry. I could tell he was pissed off by the way he screamed into the phone: "Did you see the newspaper yet? Did you see what Lincicome wrote?" I pulled the phone back within talking distance and stated that I was still in bed. Later that morning, when I got around to reading the *Chicago Tribune* sports page I was neither angry nor surprised. Columnist, Bernie Lincicome, who I had never seen at a fight in my life, had added his two cents worth to the debate of my career.

"Bodzianowski Heading for a Fall" was the headline of his April 13th column. It was a meat-ax attack on me that, among other things, compared my left jab to the action of a guy reaching across a fender to wipe a windshield. Without my prosthesis, he wrote, I was just another lumbering white fighter. With it, he added, I was just a freak in the ring whose fights were mere sideshows. About the only half flattering thing Lincicome said was that I appeared to have more tattoos than most people.

Responding to a Jack-ass like Lincicone wasn't worth the effort because, in my opinion, he was nothing more than a frustrated jock-sniffer. I heard he had gotten cut from his high school basketball team which, Lincicome included, had only five guys. He was probably a hell of a water boy in his day. I would have been happy to give him a free sample of my left jab just to set the record straight. Jerry took it more personally than I did and even contacted the moron.

Jerry Lenza: *"After several unanswered phone calls, I finally got a hold of Bernie Lincicome. I was straight and to the point with* *him. I asked him if what he meant was that every person who has faced amputation should be considered a freak. Lincicome froze, then mumbled a few words before hanging up the phone. Looking back, I am glad I connected with Lincicome on the phone instead of in person. I may have been tempted to do something I would one day regret."*

The loss to Ratliff, coupled with the stench of the Lincicome article laid me low. All it took to put me back on track was a few kind words from the NFL's all-time leading rusher.

Jerry Lenza: *"A function was being held for my friend, Ron Antos, who was involved in city politics. I received a phone call requesting me to bring Craig along. Several area athletes were scheduled to be on hand. I ran into Chicago Bear great, Walter Payton. We were discussing the Ratliff fight and Payton apologized for being unable to attend, but commented on what he heard was an excellent fight. Then the topic of the Lincicome article surfaced. Payton just shook his head and went over to talk to Craig."*

We had never met before, but I had been a Bears fan since birth. Payton wished me continued success in the ring and told me to disregard what Lincicome had written. Payton said he would have read the article except for the fact that he had stopped reading anything by Lincicome years ago.

After a few days following the fight, my attitude toward my effort started to ease. I reasoned that if I could give a rated contender hell for ten rounds, then I could duke it out with just about anyone. Personally, my leg was still a hassle at times. Following the Ratliff fight I had to go see Mike Quigley for several adjustments, but professionally I had crossed the leg barrier. By hanging with Ratliff on a near-even basis I had proved my worthiness as a fighter. I still had a score to settle with Ratliff, but first my management team suggested that I take a few tune-up bouts.

On August 30, 1987, I stepped in the ring for the first time since the Ratliff war but had no idea who I would be facing, practically up to the introductions. My opponent changed three times in the five days preceding the bout. First it was Dale Wilburn, a club fighter from Maine who pulled out because he claimed he had some drywall to finish. I've heard a million excuses for pulling out of a fight; at least Wilburn's excuse was original. Next up was Dennis Roberts of South Carolina, who all of a sudden no longer felt fit enough to compete. I had never heard of either of these guys before, and it looked like the bottom of the barrel had been scraped clean. Finally they found veteran Otis Hardy Bates from Arkansas. Bates had a not-so-impressive record of 11-9-1, and lasting almost three rounds with former IBF heavyweight champion, Tony Tucker, was the biggest accomplishment of his mediocre career.

I give Bates credit for showing up. He even charged me at the opening bell, swinging like a windmill. I ducked and nailed him to the canvas without even breaking a sweat. Quick knockouts like that do little to advance a career. I worked harder signing autographs afterwards. My family had personally sold over six hundred tickets for the fight. Leaving the dressing room after my bout, I walked past 'Smokin' Joe Frazier, whose fighter, Oliver

McCall, boxed on the undercard, while several people were hitting Frazier up for autographs. Once past Frazier, I was mobbed. Was I more popular than 'Smokin' Joe Frazier? Definitely in Chicago! I'm glad I didn't have to fight Joe for the honor.

When tragedy struck Holy Angels Catholic Church in inner city Chicago, an unlikely savior by the name of Mike Tyson came to the rescue. The church had burned down and a boxing card at DePaul Alumni Hall was held to raise funds for Pastor George Clements. Tyson was boxing an exhibition with James 'Quick' Tillis on the show. A year earlier, Tillis gave Tyson his best fight to date, dropping a close 10-round decision. I was booked to face journeyman, Al Houck, in the main supporting contest. Tyson may be no angel, but he treated me with great respect in our brief encounter. At the weigh-in he came over and shook my hand, and told me he had followed my career since the accident. Tyson was a hell of a boxing historian. He actually knew a lot more about me than I knew about him, although I recalled seeing something about him on the news recently. "Didn't you just punch out a parking lot attendant?" I asked.

Tyson gave me an embarrassed smile, put his head in his hands and said. "Nobody's perfect." Then he slapped me on the back and told me to kick Houck's ass.

Over 5,000 tickets had been sold to this event. It was speculated that most spectators were there to see Tyson. Wearing 18-ounce gloves, Tillis and Tyson gave the fans a good show. I was pleased to note that no one was leaving the auditorium as I made my way into the ring for my fight afterwards. I didn't keep them long, disposing of Houck in the second round.

Alfonzo Ratliff never did receive his promised world title shot after our bout, and had a very public divorce from Don King. King ended up dealing his contract with Ratliff for only $10, the point of which, naturally, was to humiliate the fighter even more.

> **Alfonzo Ratliff:** *"I never had any management that cared for me as a human being. Craig was fortunate. If I would have had his management team behind me, I would have retired a millionaire."*

My early blow-outs over, Bates and Houck were good confidence builders, but did little to prepare me for another bout with Ratliff. Earl Lewis provided the kind of workout I needed. The Detroit fighter was difficult to hit cleanly. When I did connect, Lewis grabbed me like an overzealous grandma. He gave me a competitive effort and lasted the distance. Lewis caught with some good shots along the way, but a bone-crunching left hand decked him in the final round to close the match in impressive fashion. My victory over Lewis occurred in February, 1988, in Chicago Heights. The weather was typical for that time of year, and before gearing up for the Ratliff rematch scheduled for April, I headed to sunny Florida for a week of shark fishing.

On the foot-front, my prosthesis had been through several recent enhancements. Mike Quigley and his associates provided me with a graphic foot that enabled me to run more each day. When I returned home I would work out twice as long in the gym and triple my morning roadwork.

The USA Network was televising the rematch. A few days before the fight, USA's boxing analyst, Sean O'Grady, paid me a visit. The last time I'd seen Sean was when we fought on the same card years earlier. Now we spent an entire day together. A film crew followed along as we visited Quigley's office and my family. Sean even accompanied me on my roadwork. He was a few years past his championship days, but he still maintained a decent fitness level.

> **Sean O'Grady:** *"At first I was skeptical, but Craig fought the same with the artificial leg as he did beforehand. After seeing him fight it would not have been fair to deny him."*

The bout was set in the southwest Chicago suburb of Harvey. Ratliff acted as if he had to fight me in my Dad's basement.

> **Alfonzo Ratliff:** *"I have fought in such far-away lands as London, England and Copenhagen, Denmark, but this environment almost seemed more hostile. I knew there would be close to 3,000 Gatormaniacs rooting against me. I was afraid of what could happen if it went to the scorecards. I requested some fight posters to hang in the black neighborhoods before the fight, and they only gave me three."*

What an exaggeration! I am sure Ratliff received at least five posters. Emotions ran high for this return engagement. Ratliff and I stood in ring center glaring deep into each other's eyes. My favorite song "Bad to the Bone" blared in the background. We returned to our respective corners and came out swinging at the bell.

The bout was staged in a small 17-foot ring—a puncher's ring. Ratliff tied me up whenever I got close. I constantly cut off the ring on him and winged left hooks. I caught Ratliff with several big right hands to take the first round and kept up my offense to clinch the second. I had learned a lot from our first go-around. This time I was slipping more of Ratliff's counter-attacks.

I came out slugging for the third round and kept pumping jabs at Ratliff whenever he got too close. Ratliff came on and landed a big uppercut. We traded shots until the end of the round. It was a close round, but the judges gave it to Ratliff.

I felt fatigued after that round. It didn't make sense. I had never run more or trained harder for a fight. This was the last thing I expected to happen. I later found out that I had actually over-trained. I had not given my body sufficient time to recuperate between double workouts and increased roadwork. It didn't bother my phony leg, but the flesh-and-blood parts of me were exhausted. There was nothing to do now but suck it up. Over the next few rounds the action see-sawed back and forth. I was digging left hooks on the inside, then moving and jabbing. I pressed Ratliff at every opportunity, but his combinations were also scoring points. We both boxed more this time, instead of trading bombs. It was close throughout.

Ratliff started to tie me up more. I kept breaking free and shooting left hooks to the body. I landed a big left uppercut near the end of the seventh. The fight was dead even up to then. I out-boxed Ratliff to take the eighth, and Sean O'Grady told the television audience that he had me slightly ahead.

Ratliff pinned me in a corner and we both punched away to start the ninth round. These last two rounds were now the most important of my career. Despite my fatigue, I pulled some reserve energy right up from the gut. I stood and traded punches, then spun out. I kept sticking my left in Ratliff's face. He countered with his own jabs and loaded up with left hooks hoping to end the fight.

Just like our first fight, the final round would be the determining factor, and I did everything I could to win it. Ratliff came out aggressively in the tenth, but I jabbed him off. Ratliff landed a big right that sent me into the ropes. I fought my way back to the center of the ring and we slugged away. A huge right hand sent me headfirst into the turnbuckle. Ratliff landed more heavy shots at the end of the round. Although near exhaustion, I stood my ground and traded punches until the final bell. We both raised our arms in victory.

Everyone in my corner told me the fight was mine. Then the announcer read the decision. One judge scored it a draw. The other two had it 46-45, and 47-44, respectively, and the announcer walked over and raised Ratliff's hand. The crowd booed and I was flabbergasted.

In the wake of my second disappointing loss, retirement briefly crossed my mind. There had to be a better and easier way to earn a living. Evander Holyfield had recently unified the cruiserweight title and then relinquished all three belts to try his luck with the heavyweights. A win over Ratliff would have qualified me for a shot at one of the vacant titles. Boxing was in my blood, but I needed some time away to sort my thoughts out.

I took several days, and one thought kept returning to mind as I weighed the pros and cons: I had proved in two fights with the former champion of the world that I belonged in the upper echelon. If I left boxing now, in my prime, I would forever wonder "What if...?" I called Jerry and told him to start planning for a Fall campaign.

FIFTEEN

You've heard the old saying, "Everyone loves a winner." I think it was invented especially for the media. The local press seemed to fall off my bandwagon the minute I lost. One article declared my dream of challenging for a world title was D.O.A. That might have been true had I been trounced by Ratliff. But that didn't happen. A lot of people thought I won the fight. Hell, if I could hang with Ratliff no one else was out of my league. I'd get another chance to prove it thanks to Holyfield's abdication of his titles. The cruiserweight division was now wide open, full of opportunities. Promoter, Alfred Marchio, from the East Coast came up with the idea for a tournament titled "Cruiser War '89." Such ranked contenders as 'Smokin' Bert Cooper, Anthony Witherspoon and Dwight Muhammad Qawi were in-and so was I.

I trained as hard as always, but this time I intended to taper down my workouts the week before the fight. Over-training had cost me once against Ratliff, and I vowed to learn from my mistake. I knew another loss at this stage in my career would push me back to the end of the line.

I had to overcome two big obstacles before I stepped into the ring against Dawud Shaw in the first round of the tournament. The first concerned Nate. He would not be coming to Philadelphia with me. His physical and mental health had deteriorated badly thanks to what was diagnosed as Alzheimer's disease. It was painfully obvious he only had a few years left. It broke my heart. I felt like something major in my life was missing. The man who'd started me out and brought me so far now couldn't enjoy the results of his work.

Fortunately, brothers Pat and Primo La Cassa, who had been involved in Chicago boxing for years, jumped in to fill in the void. They were knowledgeable boxing men and tremendous individuals, but it would take them both to fill Nate's shoes.

More annoying than anything else was the Pennsylvania boxing commission's insistence that I undergo a battery of tests to determine my fitness for the ring. That I had already done in Illinois and came through several grueling tests with flying colors, wasn't enough for these guys. So long for the popular notion in some circles that everything was greased for me along the comeback trail.

Just for fun, I decided to give myself a new look for the Pennsylvania doctors. Former world heavyweight champion, Jack Dempsey, had always been a hero of mine. I enjoyed stories about his rough-and-tumble life, and was fascinated by old pictures that showed this tough, sun-bronzed fighter who looked like he cut his own hair. As a tribute to Dempsey, I got out the shears and went to work on my own head. I left the hair on top alone, but shaved a complete circle around my noggin up to about an inch above my ears. The day before I left for Philly, I stopped by the gym and every kid there begged me to give him the same look. I charged five bucks a head and left with a wad of cash. Somehow I feel the Manassa Mauler would have approved. The 'do' was a hit in Philly, too. *The Daily News* even ran a close-up photo of it.

Maybe I wouldn't have passed the state cosmetology boards, but the medical tests they gave me in Pennsylvania were no sweat and I sailed through them with flying colors. Sporting the haircut, I passed all the tests, thumbs up. Dr. Louis Van de Beek, one of my examiners told *The Philadelphia Daily News* that my "adaptation to the artificial limb is quite remarkable. There should be no reason he shouldn't be given medical clearance to fight in Pennsylvania." A simple phone call to the Illinois commission could have told them that.

Maybe it was just a publicity stunt to hype interest in the tournament. Promoters certainly weren't above that sort of thing, and when I saw the fight posters around town I just rolled my eyes. Dwight Muhammad Qawi and Anthony Witherspoon got top billing. That was understandable; Qawi was a former world champion, and Witherspoon was a local boxer and ranked contender. Under my name all it said was "amputee." Well, if it helped put asses in seats on fight night, fine. At least my name had been spelled right.

My first-round opponent in the tournament on November 24th, was Dawud Shaw. Because I'd committed myself to an early December bout back home, my plan was to take him out fast. I was a bit overanxious in the beginning, but I calmed down and centered my attack on Shaw's body. Eventually he crumbled, giving me a late round knockout. The second round of the tournament was slated for February 15, 1989, again in Philadelphia.

However, I still had to face Andre Crowder back in Chicago just two weeks after the Shaw victory.

I should have taken my time, or a vacation. My performance against Andre Crowder was one of my most disappointing. I felt flat and did barely enough to win. The judges actually called it an eight-round draw, which surprised me as much as it did at the end of round seven to learn that the fight wasn't scheduled for 10 rounds. For the last few years most of my matches had been 10-rounders. The original contract for the Crowder match said it was a tenner. Even the ring announcer that night said "10 rounds or less." But, then at the end of the seventh, they announced it was the last round coming up. Like I said, I wasn't my top self that night anyway, and the fight was close. I had figured that I still had three rounds to pull it out. I won the eighth easily enough, and when the decision was announced. I could only shake my head. Crowder and I were not finished.

A few weeks later I was back in Philadelphia, but not to hit anybody. The Philadelphia Sports Writers' Association was holding its 85th annual banquet honoring athletes from around the country for various accomplishments. I had been named recipient of the "Most Courageous Athlete," an honor that made me very proud. I was told that I could bring a date to the banquet, and since my mom did not get a chance to travel much, I asked her. It wasn't just because I wanted to have the best-looking date in the joint. I had a little surprise planned for her. Jerry came with us, too.

The awards banquet was set for January 30, 1989, at the Hyatt in Cherry Hill. They had told me that once I accepted my award I would have to give a speech. Jerry and my mom constantly asked what I had planned to talk about, but I told them it was a secret. I did throw them a little hint, explaining that my idea of courage was probably different than what they expected.

Such remarkable athletes as former Pittsburgh Steeler runningback, Rocky Bleier, and former Los Angeles Dodger pitching ace, Tommy John, had received my award in past years, so it was nothing to be taken frivolously. I knew I was now included in a special group. After Jackie Joyner-Kersee accepted the "Outstanding Athlete", I was called to the podium for my award. I looked out at the elegantly dressed wall-to-wall crowd and after a few light remarks, started speaking right from the heart. I felt it was important to first define the word "courage." I opened up a dictionary and recited the definition: "Courage is the attitude or response of facing or dealing with anything recognized as dangerous, difficult, or painful. Instead of withdrawing from it, it is the quality of being fearless or brave." Then I explained to everyone my own feelings on the subject.

"Courage," I said, "is a man and a woman, a marriage with six children, four boys and two girls, the death of one son, and the loss of a leg by another. To overcome, that is courage. I gladly accept this award on behalf of my mom and dad, Gloria and Pat Bodzianowski." I made eye contact with my mother. It was a tremendous feeling to see her look so proud. My boxing comeback took some guts, I guess, but mostly I was just pig-headed enough to want to continue my life according to my own design. My parents had both exhibited plenty of courage in the way they raised their large family and endured hardships and heartbreaks. Getting good parents is purely luck of the draw, and I'd hit the jackpot in that lotto.

Gloria Bodzianowski: *"Craig's speech was one of the highlights of his career. There was not* *a dry eye in the place. It was my first time to Philadelphia and I will never forget it".*

Before we left Philadelphia, I spotted a poster advertising my next fight in "Cruiser War 89." I was slated to face William Sanders, identified as a cruiserweight from New Jersey. I was again listed as an amputee. It was time to prove to East Coast fans that I was a legitimate contender and not a gimmick to sell tickets.

Qawi and Witherspoon were the tournament favorites. Dwight had twice KO'd local favorite, Matthew Saad Muhammad, in light heavyweight title bouts. He'd gone up to 240 pounds to fight George Foreman who stopped him. But the fact that Qawi dropped 50 pounds to fight in "Cruiser War '89" was an indication of how serious he was about reclaiming past glory. As for Witherspoon, his biggest booster was his brother Tim, who'd twice held a slice of the heavyweight title and boasted to anyone who would listen that Anthony would easily win the tournament.

Nobody predicted I would win it; the betting was that I'd fall as soon as I faced one of the world-ranked entries. And maybe even to my next opponent, who turned out not to be the advertised Willie Saunders, who'd withdrawn due to injury, but Andre Crowder, who'd held me to a draw two months earlier.

That had been a fluke, and this time the decision about how long the fight would go was going to be up to me. In the gym I practiced throwing shorter, compact right hands, and I also dropped ten pounds with my heavy training regimen.

February 16th was a difficult night for "Cruiser War '89," but a memorable evening for me. One of the local heroes, 'Smokin' Bert Cooper, was eliminated from the tournament after suffering a late-round knockout defeat to Nate Miller. Dwight Muhammad Qawi stayed alive after eking out a hairline decision over Tyrone Booze. Anthony Witherspoon pounded out a hard fought twelve-round decision over Bash Ali, capturing the vacant World Boxing Association Americas crown in the process. Most importantly, justice would be served in my rematch with Crowder.

The Philly press had been on my case about a power shortage in my right hand. On February 16th, I answered the critics-and settled a score-by splitting Crowder's eye open with the punch I'd worked on in the gym. Blood spurted everywhere and the match was stopped in the second round. My only response to that particular reporter was, "If I have problems with getting power behind my right tonight, I hope I always have that problem."

The biggest loser of the night was probably Alfredo Marchio, the promoter. In spite of having some big-name boxers and a one-legged wonder on the bill, the Civic Center was only half filled for the fights. On top of that, most of the bouts went the distance, forcing Marchio to purchase expensive additional satellite time for the pay-per-view broadcast of the card. Rumors surfaced that the rest of the tournament would be scrapped, but eventually Marchio decided to keep the scheduled April date for the semi-finals. My opponent would be the favorite, Anthony Witherspoon. After four years and twelve fights on a prosthesis, I was ready to stand among the elite in the cruiserweight division.

I honestly felt that I would have advanced to this point in my career a few years earlier had it not been for the accident. Now the issue was no longer my leg; that had long since been resolved. I deserved to be remembered more than just the guy who fought on after losing a leg. I never considered it to be a major accomplishment. Defeating Anthony Witherspoon would be something to be excited about, guaranteeing me a world ranking and strong consideration for a world title attempt.

The semi-finals of "Cruiser War '89" were switched to Scranton. I was in the hotel restaurant the morning of the fight when Witherspoon's brother, "Terrible Tim," got in my face. "You want nothing to do with my brother, man!" he barked. I leaped up and met him eyeball-to-eyeball.

"You can step in line right after your brother, and if you've got anymore brothers, I'll fight them, too!" I shot back. Then I sat down and finished breakfast. Nobody else bothered me; people obviously wanted nothing to do with this crazy Polack,

The Witherspoons weren't done with their games. At the weigh-in I came in at exactly the contracted weight Witherspoon and his stooges claimed I was actually a half-pound over. Tournament supervisor, Marty Cohen, had seen enough from them. "If he takes that leg off he'll be way under the maximum weight limit," he snapped, closing the subject. Although in his mid-eighties, Cohen was one of those old-timers who commanded respect and always received it. No one from the Witherspoon entourage responded. Cohen grabbed me before exiting the weigh-in and wished me well. He was obviously angered from their classless display.

The fight was scheduled for 12 rounds, because Witherspoon's WBA Americas title was on the line. I had never fought that long before, and I didn't intend to start now. I was in Witherspoon country, and couldn't count on getting a decision.

As challenger, I was first to enter the ring. When he got there, Witherspoon flashed his shiny belt in my direction.

It only made me want it more. I had plenty of supporters in the house, and their cheers energized me. I was the underdog, which didn't bother me. I intended to perform like a pitbull.

Witherspoon was highly skilled. He slipped most of my opening shots and countered with his own. He was a master at feints and head movements which confused me in the early going. I kept pressing ahead when all of a sudden Witherspoon landed a right that sent me staggering into the rope and then bouncing to the canvas. My head was spinning. I stayed on one knee for the entire eight-count, attempting to clear my head. I even looked over to my corner and winked to make it look good. Witherspoon bought my possum routine and was cautious when the action resumed. I moved away from him while the fog lifted in my head. Witherspoon continued to score from long range, and won the opening session by a wide margin.

With my head clear again, I began the second round boxing instead of pursuing Witherspoon. Nice try, Gator. All I got for my trouble was another three-minute leather facial. Nothing was working. One of my life's major opportunities was slipping away. TV analyst Michael Marley told the pay-per- view audience that, "Bodzianowski may have stepped too far out of his class in this one."

Pat LaCassa told me to take the fight to Witherspoon again, and I came out for the third knowing I needed to win the round to get back into the match. I went downstairs, landing left hooks to Witherspoon's mid-section. He answered back with plenty of potent blows of his own, but adrenaline had kicked in and his punches no longer had the same effect. The tide was turning in my direction.

Throughout the middle rounds, my incessant body attack steadily slowed Witherspoon down. I'd eaten my share of punches and both my eyes were dark and swollen. Going into the eleventh, my corner had me slightly ahead but told me I must win the last two rounds. "Remember this, he's the champ and this is Pennsylvania!" Pat said. It was the moon, or some other place I'd never gone before, as far as I was concerned.

After 10 rounds, I was drained, and Witherspoon seemed somehow to have regenerated. For every one I landed in the eleventh, I got two in return. No matter what I did, Witherspoon did it better. I knew I'd blown the round as I wearily made my way back to my corner. It all came down to the next three minutes. That's a lifetime when you're exhausted, but I had been through hell to get there, and if both my legs fell off now I was still going out there and doing my best.

I stuck a jab in Witherspoon's face to start the final round and never looked back. I put fatigue out of my head and let my heart take over. After every combination I threw, I took a breath and started its successor on the way, and told myself to keep it up until Witherspoon fell or I heard a bell.

"We have a close but unanimous decision," intoned the announcer Ed Darian. Oh shit, I thought, wishing we were in Chicago. "Judge Buddy Rusch scores it 114-113, Judge John McHale has it 114-110, and, finally, Jack Castelloni has it 114-113 for the winner and new-WBA Americas Champion, Craig Bodzianowski!"

I jumped into the air, finally a champion of something beyond Illinois, and on my way to even bigger dreams. I had just beaten one of the world's top cruiserweights, and that made poor, crippled, thick-headed Craig Bodzianowski one of the best.

I was so euphoric that when Marley asked in the post-fight interviews whether I thought I should now be considered more than a carnival act, I didn't rip his face off but suggested he ask Witherspoon about that. Then I looked straight into the live camera and said, "To all my critics who said it couldn't be done...!" and I put my thumb on my nose, wagged my fingers and blew a raspberry.

Unfortunately, The public reacted to the promotion the same way. Promoter, Alfredo Marchio, took another financial pounding and, the finals of "Cruiser War 89" were scrapped. I had been scheduled to face Qawi. He contacted Jerry about rescheduling the bout in Chicago, but then he priced himself out of the equation. By the end of the year, Qawi got a shot and lost it to WBA champion, Robert 'Little Joe' Daniels. That my turn was coming seemed evident to even those who had doubted me before.

"Bodzianowski in Contention for Title Shots"...read the headline in the September 7th *Chicago Tribune*. The brief article reported that, on the strength of my stunning upset over Anthony Witherspoon earlier in the year, Tinley Park amputee, Craig Bodzianowski, had cracked the top ten rankings of the World Boxing Association and International Boxing Federation, and was expected to get a try at one of their belts.

Although I had reached my goal of attaining world class contender status, I needed another dream to put me out on the edge again. I focused my intensity on a march toward the world title. Not bad for a guy whom many had once doubted would ever fight again.

SIXTEEN

It was no time to just sit around and wait. I had to stay active so that when the time came I'd be ready.

Jaime "The Featherman" Howe was a former Toughman battler with a reputation as a face-first slugger, my favorite type of opponent. Howe had looked impressive in decision losses to former champions, Don LaLonde and Dennis Andries, and I looked for a good test from him when we fought. But Howe pulled out at the last minute, leaving the promotion at Chicago's International Amphitheatre up in the air with thousands of tickets having been sold. If the show was scrapped it would cost plenty, not only money but fan goodwill as well. I asked Jerry to find a credible substitute right away. He contacted Florida-based promoter, Mike Acri, who delivered once defeated James Warring of West Virginia.

Warring was a former three-time world champion kick-boxer now dedicating himself to boxing. The fact that he had been a successful kick-boxer didn't alarm me. If he used his feet in our fight, I'd take my leg off and hit him over the head with it.

The only thing Warring used his feet for was to run away from me. The guy turned out to be a better runner then Carl Lewis. I chased him for ten rounds. Only rarely would he stop flitting and fire punches. I had trouble catching him and at the conclusion of the uneventful rounds I knew it was close. Neither one of us had established a clean advantage. It was one boring game of cat-and-mouse. I was the cat, Warring was the mouse, and the judges were rats. They voted 46-44, 47-46, and 46-45 in favor of Warring. I couldn't believe it. I didn't have a mark on me; you couldn't even tell I had been in a fight. It was a kick in the head, all right.

> **Jerry Lenza:** *"The bout was extremely close. The judges saw it one way and our corner saw it another way. I felt the fight was real tight going into the 9th round, but Craig picked up the tempo and won the final two stanzas. I take nothing away from Warring. He did what he had to do. I thought Craig was the aggressor and deserved the nod."*

The WBA had rated me number five before the Warring farce. After the setback I fell to number nine. I still qualified for world title consideration. So did Warring. Less than two years later, he captured the IBF cruiserweight title by knocking out James Pritchard in the first round. I guess he finally discovered what the hands are for in traditional boxing.

On March 13, 1990, I got knocked out. Not by Bruce Johnson, who I demolished in two rounds, but by the woman I was introduced to after the fight by a mutual friend. Her name was Sheila Desonia, and she was quite different from the women I had previously known. At first glance I found her to be attractive and charismatic, but there was more about her that grabbed me. She was smart, and goal-oriented. She was working on her higher education. We hit it off from the beginning. Sheila wasn't interested in riding the Gator bandwagon. She was attracted to me as a complete person. She was a keeper in every way, and became my wife.

Everything was coming together. Mike Acri phoned Jerry about the possibility of a title shot. Acri had WBA cruiserweight champion, Robert Daniels, under contract and thought I'd be a worthwhile and marketable challenger. Acri had Seattle, Washington in mind for the fight, which was great with me. I'd never been there before, but Seattle was almost like a hometown for me. My foot was born there.

Mine was one of two world title fights on what Acri called "The Seattle Showdown," on July 19th at the Kingdome. It would be the biggest extravaganza held in the city since heavyweight champ, Floyd Patterson, knocked out Pete Radamacher on August 22, 1957. Radamacher was the Olympic gold medalist the year before that, and when he stepped into the ring for his shot at the world championship, he had never fought as a professional before. Some guys have all the luck. The promotion included more than fisticuffs. It was to be a weekend-long wingding at which Muhammad Ali would be honored as "Fighter of the Century," at a $250-per-plate testimonial dinner. There would be a black-tie cocktail cruise aboard the "Spirit of Puget Sound" at $200 a head.

Pat and Primo LaCassa put me through a boot-camp-like training program unlike anything I'd experienced before. I'd never get another try at the world title, and we left nothing to chance. Daniels was a slick boxer, and I needed to be ready to slip his punches. Toward that end, we stretched a rope across the ring at shoulder height. For an hour every day I'd duck and bob under it. I sparred with quick smaller boxers like Ron Amundson who'd been in with renowned middleweights, Roy Jones and James Toney. No way was Robert Daniels as fast as Amundson. As the weeks went by, my timing improved and I started catching Amundson with a higher percentage of punches.

Everything was going almost too smoothly—but then normalcy returned like a kick in the teeth, or in this case, ribs. One morning as I rolled out of bed, I doubled over from a sharp pain in my rib cage. I could barely hobble out of the house.. I took a few days off from training, hoping whatever was wrong would heal itself. I guess I had bruised my ribs in a sparring session. I couldn't believe my bad luck. At the pinnacle of my career, everything I had worked so hard for was suddenly in jeopardy. If I pulled out of the fight, it would have been over for me. So I kept my mouth shut about the injury. I laid off sparring for a week and then, when I could move a little better, used a rib protector.

One of the best things about being in Seattle was my reunion with the makers of the Seattle Foot. Don and Shirley Poggi and their crew at Model + Instrument Development were fantastic. They were more than hospitable--Don gave me the new, improved prosthesis to use in the fight. It was lighter than my other devices, and that could only help me in the ring.

> ***Don Poggi:*** *"Craig was a pioneer by raising expectations of amputees on what they might expect to do with their lives after receiving a*

prosthesis. His heavy workload on the prosthesis fueled a desire for more high-tech improvements. It had been rare for amputees to be so active until Craig set the wave in motion as a highly visible person returning back to his normal occupation. Today technology has advanced the prosthetic industry. We now have more advanced equipment like the electronic knee. The bar in this industry was raised by determined people like Craig. He always represented himself and my company in such a positive manner. My industry will always be grateful for what he accomplished for himself and for the mind set of thousands of amputees."

One of my best experiences was a boat cruise with Don and Shirley and their employees. I couldn't believe how excited they were about the fight. I was quite amused to board the boat and see how everyone was dressed in homemade red 'Gator' shirts. Their constant support meant so much to me. They had an assortment of banners made up and were handing out little plastic alligators.

Of course the press was out in force, and I ate my usual diet of questions about my leg. I was used to that, but some of their queries almost made me laugh out loud. What was my prediction for the fight, someone asked. Did they expect me to say that I expected to get my head handed to me? "I feel confident of victory," I deadpanned.

"Why?" one pencil-necked geek asked in an annoying tone.

"Because I eat better, train harder, and I have better breeding," I said.

He bit. "Better breeding?" he inquired in a puzzled manner.

"Yeah," I said, "I'm a hard-headed Polack."

They got me back. *The Seattle Times* ran a detailed story that mentioned I still occasionally rode a motorcycle. When my parents saw it, Daniels was the last of my worries.

At the testimonial dinner for Muhammad Ali, the guest of honor pulled me aside and wished me luck. All the fighters were given the opportunity to present their thoughts on Ali and on the upcoming fights.

> ***Jerry Lenza:*** *"Tony Tucker, the former IBF heavyweight champion, made a touching speech on Ali. He also went into detail on his association with Craig and the time they competed on the same card in Chicago. It was a touching gesture which added to the program. Craig was receiving an enormous amount of attention in Seattle based on his title shot. It was more than he ever planned on. Another guest speaker, seated next to Ali was Mike Tyson's manager, Bill Cayton. Cayton drew the attention of his audience by declaring, 'The idea of a man with one leg fighting for a world title defies description. It is extraordinary. It makes truth seem stranger than fiction.'"*

The day of the fight, I attended Mass with my brother, Howard, and then rested in my hotel room before going to the Kingdome. I had complete confidence in myself as I headed to the biggest event of my life.

At the weigh-in, I jumped on the scale fully clothed, and still came in comfortably under the 190-pound limit. I wanted Daniels to see that I'd paid my dues in camp and was in prime condition. The champion, on the other hand, had to strip naked to make it to the division limit. That told me that he could be weakened from a struggle to make weight. We were fitted with the gloves we would wear later that day in the ring. Mexican-style Reyes brand gloves were the choice, and I could not have been happier. They're smaller, and the padding is distributed more towards the back of the glove, making it advantageous for the puncher—in this case, me. Then the media asked Daniels and me to pose for pictures. We stood next to each other but never exchanged words or shook hands. I saved those type of activities for after the contest.

During the preliminary matches I would occasionally pop my head out of the dressing room to view some fight action. You could tell this was a high-class event just by the ring card girls. W-O-W! The cheers for them were almost as loud as the crowd's reaction each time Ali took a bow from his ringside seat.

As the challenger I was the first contestant called to the ring. I loosened up and paced around waiting for Daniels. I looked out in the crowd and noticed that directly behind Ali was the contingent from Model + Instrument Development, waving the largest red-and- white "Gator!" banner ever made.

Daniels entered the ring wearing star-spangled shorts and waving a pair of small American flags. He was either displaying his patriotism or imitating Apollo Creed. He danced around the ring loosening up.

It was time to catch my dream. I came out pressuring Daniels. He was slick, though, darting in and out and showing me quick side-to-side movement. I got him against the ropes and opened up with both hands. My right had been my favorite weapon of late, and I scored well with it. I set him up for the right by snapping out crisp jabs. The first round was mine. The title was only eleven rounds away.

In the second, it and I went in opposite directions. I came out forcing the action again as Daniels attempted to box from a distance. Whenever we moved in close, Daniels punched to my body. And that's when he caught me with the most damaging blow of my entire career and the one that ended my chances of returning to Chicago as champion of the world. An uppercut found the damaged area of my ribs and I could feel the ribs move and pop out of position. It hurt so bad that as I walked back to my corner at the bell, I looked down to see if a rib or two was sticking out. I wasn't about to quit, but it was all I could do to move around.

The next few rounds were competitive enough, featuring some entertaining exchanges. But, every time I fired the right, the pain knocked the wind out of me. I stayed in pursuit of Daniels but soaked up my share of punishment along the way. For the balance of the fight the one-legged challenger was little more than one armed, too.

When Daniels' hand was raised, my heart ached even worse than my damaged ribs. I had given everything I could, and leaving the ring without the title belt around my waist was a crushing disappointment. I felt I had let everyone down, and it was a long, dark walk back to my dressing room.

There I was greeted by Don Poggi. I appreciated the way he and his gang had rolled out the red carpet for me all weekend and I had hoped to repay them for it and for their help in getting me back on two feet again by bringing home the title. But I had failed, and there didn't seem to be anything left to say. Don gave me a little lesson in perspective.

He told me that I had been a great asset not only to his company and the entire prosthetic industry, but had also proved to many handicap individuals the difference a positive attitude can make. I demonstrated that it was possible for a world-class athlete to return to his chosen sport after amputation. He said. My performance in the past years had changed the entire outlook on the amputee industry. The focus was now on ways to get amputees back into society as normal individuals instead of treating them like geriatrics.

It is amazing nowadays what some people have accomplished despite supposedly insurmountable odds. To think that I might've played a role in it is very gratifying. In recent years, several books for amputees have been published to help them deal with their situations. One such book, published in 1995 and titled, "You're Not Alone", deals with personal issues facing amputees and features amazing stories about several amputees. I think books like these help people cope. When I was hurt I didn't have that luxury, only blind ambition. Helping the prosthetic world was never my initial goal, but looking back I'm glad I could help. I do know one thing; no one before me physically abused a prosthesis as much as I did. I went through several models, suggesting ideas along the way for various improvements. Prosthetics have become lighter in weight and more flexible in recent years. That, and advanced socket designs and high-tech componentry have expanded the possibilities for amputees.

Poggi's consoling words made me realize that in the game of life I had been victorious, and that my defeat in the championship match was only minor in comparison. The fact that I persevered to qualify for the shot was a championship feat in itself.

Don Poggi: *"It's not a magic or bionic foot that allows an amputee to achieve the potential of a full-bodied human being. That is determined by the individual, and Craig proved what could be possible with determination. Craig's efforts set the wave in motion for the increasing level of amputees returning back to a normal life."*

SEVENTEEN

Three months after my title challenge, I returned to action in Chicago, decisioning Oscar Holman in eight rounds. But I wasn't long for the squared circle.

There were more high points, including a two-bout series in Marseilles, France in the spring of 1991. I won both fights, but got more out of the mandatory pre-fight brain scan. The doctor showed me actual pictures of the inside of my head and contrary to the claims of some friends and family members, there was no hamster on a treadmill. It was a relief to see that my brain was unmarked by the shots I had taken in my career. I must have a hard head, because nobody ever knocked me out. My punch wasn't too bad, either, since it put twenty-three of my opponents to sleep.

After I stopped Jordan Keepers back in Illinois in 1993, I thought about putting it in gear for another title quest. I was in heavy training when I was stricken with several prosthetic related injuries. It got so that my nub ached too much for me to even walk with my artificial leg. Finally, I had to have the bone cut and fixed. It was months before I could even put on a prosthesis, and all the momentum I had regained came to a screeching halt. After eleven years as a prize-fighter, it was time to explore other avenues in life.

During the layoff, several major changes occurred in my life. I became a family man. Sheila gave birth to our first child, a son named Kenneth Gator Bodzianowski. For the first time since I could remember, boxing was no longer the top priority in my life.

We had our dream house built in 1993, in the southwest Chicago suburb of Frankfort. My log cabin home sits on several acres, and with its rural setting you would think you were in the woods of northern Wisconsin. The property includes a large garage that I plan to convert someday into my own boxing gym.

I took over my dad's tattoo shop, Pat's Tattoos, in Lockport, Illinois. Running a tattoo parlor is a tough racket. I owned the business for a little over five years. My dad had once made a decent buck running the place, but the secret was out, and tattoo shops were springing up on every street corner. Some days I made a lot of money and others I made less than it cost to heat the place. I enjoyed being my own boss, but the profits were too inconsistent. In early '99 I closed the doors of Pat's Tattoos. I had hoped to persuade eccentric Dennis Rodman to come in for some work while he was a Chicago Bull, but it never happened. He alone might have kept me going for another year or two.

I have some ideas for a new business venture. I still love training pit bulls, and there's a new market for them as protection for new property developments. The dogs are dropped off in the evening in new vacant housing units and then picked up early the next morning. Any burglar or vandal who enters one of these guarded homes soon wishes he hadn't. Trust me, nobody wants to mess with a trained pit bull. I'm toying with the idea of getting a fleet of these canine Gators ready for action.

In the meantime I have become domesticated. A few years ago the Bodzianowski household got another addition when my daughter, Paige, was born. I cook just about every meal for my two kids. I've always enjoyed cooking wild game and have recently added many recipes to my portfolio. Barbecued ribs are a house favorite. My son loves them so much he could eat them for every meal. When he recently received an outstanding grade in school, for a reward, Kenny requested barbecued ribs and creamed potatoes for breakfast. I obliged. Now every time he does a good deed he wants to be compensated with barbecued ribs and creamed potatoes.

Life after boxing has been good to me. It was hard when I lost Nate and my father, two influential human beings in my life. Believe me, the amputation of a leg is minor compared to the loss of a loved one. I try to use the lessons and knowledge passed down from Nate and my father. Dad was strict but fair. I use his principles when raising my own. Mostly, I try to pass on the confidence and work ethic my father instilled in me.

Occasionally, my name appears in various publications. Not too long ago, *The Ring* magazine had an article in which a select group of boxers talked about the hardest punch they ever landed. Robert Daniels cited a right hand he landed against my jaw. It's the one he landed to my side that I remember most, but I consider Daniels' remark a tribute to my chin. I took his best punch and didn't fall.

The July 1998 addition of *The Ring* carried an article on handicapped golfer, Casey Martin, whose use of a golf cart on the PGA Tour had caused a big flap. Martin suffers from a circulatory problem in one of his legs that is compounded by walking. But the golf bigwigs said his cart gave Martin an unfair advantage over the ambulatory hackers.

Ring correspondent, Pete Ehrmann, phoned for my perspective on the matter. I thought they should give the kid a chance. Martin proved he had the ability to be on the tour. A golf cart didn't improve his golf game anymore than a prosthesis improved my fighting ability. Sometimes, exceptions need to be made.

I guess the best advice I can share with anyone facing long odds is to not be afraid to fail. There is a certain comfort level that comes with being mediocre, because this is the category most people fall into. Winning takes guts. Not trying is a guaranteed way to avoid success. Never be paralyzed by the fear of failure. For some people, one sure way to prevent failure is to never try.

I never believed in labels that other people tried to put on me. I am not a handicapped individual. If I were, I would take advantage of the sticker and choose the parking pass I was once offered. Attitude means everything. I truly believe I can do most activities better than anyone else. The *only* difference is, one of my legs is manufactured. Frankly, if someone calls me handicapped to my face, he risks being punched in the mouth.

My boxing career resumed in spite of my disadvantage, because I was surrounded by a winning cast, people who truly had my best interest at heart. My family, my boxing associates, and my friends believed in me and provided a wealth of positive motivation. Whenever I needed their support, I knew it would be available.

I learned many positive lessons along the way. I realized fantasies never come true, because it's the commitment to success that determines the final results. It was after a lot of hardship that I finally learned how to walk, and eventually train, with a prosthesis. Quitting was never an option.

I have been blessed in many ways. This world can be a cruel place. Rising above it ain't easy, but Thomas Edison probably put it best when he said, "Genius is 10% inspiration and 90% perspiration." In boxing we say it a little differently: "Keep your ass off the floor and keep punching." No matter what others say, believe in yourself, know your individual abilities count. Winners don't always take the top prize, but they get to play in the game, and that makes all the difference in the world.